# STREET-SMART PERSUASION

A Speaker's Guide
To Socratic Design

VICKI GOODFELLOW DUKE

**Kendall Hunt**
publishing company

Cover image © Shutterstock.com

www.kendallhunt.com
*Send all inquiries to:*
4050 Westmark Drive
Dubuque, IA 52004-1840

Published in the United States of America

# Directory

# WHY STREET-SMART?

Speakers today need to be street-smart and savvy. Contemporary culture presents challenges to traditional notions of persuasion and invites us to take a fresh look at the tools necessary to exert influence in the twenty-first century.

This text proposes a unique and unconventional design for persuasive messaging. Research in cognitive science, neuroscience, communication theory and psychology supports the theory on which this structure is based and points to optimal design choices for mastery in the art of influence.

**Here are four ways in which this text is different from traditional persuasive texts, followed by two problems and one big bold claim.**

1. **Focus on Persuasive *Speaking*:** Persuasion is not a one-size-fits-all objective. The rules of persuasion vary according to the mode of delivery. Written and spoken messaging are different and need to be treated as two distinct objectives. This text focuses on persuasion as it applies to oral delivery.

2. **Socratic Design**: Socratic design is the strongest indicator for successful persuasive messaging outcomes. The Socratic approach rejects conclusion explicitness and increases audience engagement.

3. **Street-Smart Logic versus Formal Logic**: While knowledge of formal logic may be useful, it has some serious limitations. Because the average person on the street is not schooled in formal logic, arguments which rely on the use of formal logic often miss the mark. It is akin to speaking in a language foreign to your listeners and expecting results. In most contemporary contexts, we need other tools to reach our audiences.

4. **Focus on Everyday Practice:** There is no need to wait for a live audience to practice persuasive speaking. Daily life provides ample opportunities to hone skills. Techniques and strategies can be implemented every day in both our ordinary and extraordinary conversations. The more frequently we use skills, the more quickly they become habits. The ability to exert influence, personally and professionally can become a habit.

© Yuravector/Shutterstock.com

**Now, let's look at two very common communication problems:**

1. People often have difficulty recalling content of informative messages.

2. People often fail to take action following persuasive appeals.

Let's acknowledge that these are broad sweeping statements which would be difficult to gauge with any kind of metric precision; however, it will be easy for most of us to confirm these statements from our personal experiences alone, both in interpersonal and public communications.

It may even be suggested that the success rate for both of these types of messaging is staggeringly low. Why?

Now for the big, bold claim:

**We have been looking at informative message design and persuasive message design backward, as far as the intent of end goals.**

Studies in cognitive science help us to understand the problem and point us to a solution, if we pay attention. When we do pay attention and re-frame our thinking on message design, the results change dramatically. This author has noted significant and consistent change in persuasive perception outcomes, over the course of twenty-five years of teaching and coaching speakers, when Socratic Design framing is used in comparison with traditional persuasive message design.

Let's look at the problems inherent in the traditional design of informative and persuasive messages.

Traditionally, the teaching on informative messaging is that one is to provide information for the purpose of creating awareness alone, not to demand an action (take-away, ask, call to action) as an end goal.

Conversely, the expectation in persuasive messaging is to demand a call to action.

But this is wrong.

Here is why this thinking is problematic.

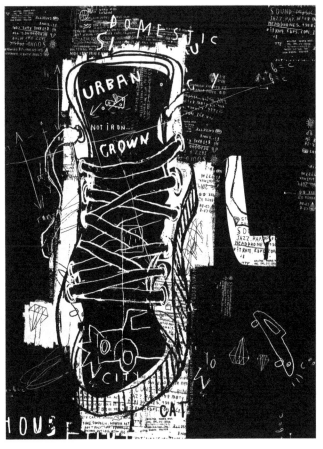

© Dmitriip/Shutterstock.com

When we deliver an informative message, it is because we believe the recipients of the message _need that information_ for some reason. Think about it. We do not tell people things they don't need to know.

Imagine that you have been asked to present a new policy to a group of colleagues. Why? Why have you been asked to tell them this information? Because someone thinks they _need the information._

Now, here is the step where we need to dig more deeply. Why do they need the information? If you ask your boss why the group needs this information, he will likely respond that they need it so that _the next time they apply for benefits, they will know what to do_. This is an _action_.

Contrary to popular belief, we don't tell people things only for them to have "awareness." We tell people things because we want them to _use_ that awareness in a particular way.

Why do you tell your partner that the cream has expired? So they are "aware"? Yes, but you want them to take this awareness and _do_ something with it. You might want them to throw the cream away. You might want them to offer to go to the grocery store. You want them to _do_ something.

Let's use a more social example. You may believe that you share a video of a cute puppy on social media so that your friend will be "aware" of how cute the puppy is; but really, why do you want them to be aware? You want them to be aware so that they _like_ the post, _share_ the video, _tell_ a friend, or simply _appreciate_ the cuteness of puppies. Those are all _actions_.

_We inform people so they will take some kind of action._ Remember that an action can be physical (try, sing, do further research) or cognitive (remember, consider, imagine, etc.) **Informative Messages Demand Action.**

Now, let's look at persuasion and the traditional call to action which appears at the end of a message. Historically, we have been told to have a clear call to action at the end, such as "sign this petition," or "start riding horses," or "Vote Separatist party"!

This request for action often fails to produce the intended results and here is the reason why: Persuasion itself is a process. Theorists agree that persuasion is not a one time event, but a gradual process (Azjen and Fishbein 1975; Azjen 1991; Roskos-Ewoldsen 1997; Rhodes and Roskos-Ewoldsen 2013). Oftentimes persuasive messages are 5 minutes long, or even 30 minutes long, yet following the message we expect people to vote differently, to believe in a higher power, to study abroad! We are asking too much in too short of a period. Our expectations are unrealistic.

**The goal of any persuasive message should be to get people thinking in a new way and to leave them with a valuable <u>seed</u> of information that will grow and flourish when the time is right.** The time indeed may be today, but more often than not, it will be three weeks from now, three months from now, or three years from now. What will make the greatest impact in exerting influence is if we can encourage *mental elaboration* from the audience. We want the audience to think about our ideas when we leave the room. We want the audience to be aware of something so powerful that it changes the way they see the world, so that the seed we have planted will take root when the time is just right.

Therefore, the end goal of an **informative message** should be to **ask for a specific action**, while the goal of a **persuasive appeal** should be to **plant a seed** that has the potential to grow and flourish.

Onward, to persuasive message design, the Socratic way.

# STREET-TALK:
# THE POWER
# OF QUESTIONS

*The questions we ask ourselves
will shape the lives that we lead.*

# Socratic Dialogue

The Socratic Method is a method of inquiry designed to elicit a truth.

Socrates taught his followers not through explicit statements (informative structure), but by asking sequential questions which would provoke critical thinking and reasoning skills in his listeners, leading them to discover truths through this guided process.

While research continues to emerge on Socratic design in oral persuasive messaging, the Socratic Method itself is a time-tested, well-respected pedagogical method used in many liberal arts universities and law schools internationally.

In its purest form, the Socratic Method is a process by which a questioner directs pointed questions to a specific listener, addressing them by name and expects a direct response in return.

In a public speaking context, this method will take the form of Socratic dialogue.

In Socratic dialogue, the questioner, or speaker, will guide the audience collectively, rather than individually, through a series of predetermined questions to allow them to consider data and to reach their own conclusion (Jowett, 2010; Paul, and Elder 2007).

Below is a brilliant example of Socratic Design in action, being used to solve a real-world problem. The story is taken from *Power of Moments* by Chip and Dan Heath (Trip over the Truth: 1)

Once you read this story, you will never forget it.

https://bit.ly/SocraticD

# Question Framing

Instead of using an explicit statement at the beginning of a persuasive argument, use a **nonleading question, or a question which does not give away your position. Avoid conclusion explicitness.**

This approach is likely in contrast to what you are accustomed to seeing in persuasive speeches; however, the evidence suggests that this method is more effective for a number of reasons: Question Framing or Socratic Design is a superior design because it *prevents bias, increases audience engagement* and *respects human autonomy.*

Framing a controversial topic as a **nonleading question** is more effective than conclusion explicitness in eliciting positive persuasive responses (Hovland and Mandell 1952;

S. Brehm and J. Brehm 1981; Niederdeppe et al. 2012). The strength of this position will become more evident as we examine, in subsequent chapters, the role of pre-existing attitudes in persuasive messaging outcomes.

While avoiding conclusion explicitness is suggested here, we must briefly consider the data which oppose this viewpoint. Discrepant findings in favor of conclusion explicitness were found only in studies which examined advertising messaging (O'Keefe 1997; Cruz 1998) or noncontroversial messaging. It should be noted that much of the research supporting conclusion explicitness was conducted on written persuasive messaging as opposed to *oral* persuasive messaging. The oral modality poses unique demands which must be considered for successful outcomes.

The success of an oral persuasive appeal relies heavily on audience engagement. A positiive correlation is noted in the aforementioned studies, between framing the topic as a nonleading question, avoiding conclusion explicitness and increased audience engagement. Viewing these findings through the lens of the Elaboration Likelihood Model, (Petty and Cacciopo 1986) it may be suggested that omitting an explicit conclusion at the beginning of a speech increases cognitive elaboration and therefore engagement.

# Prevent Bias

**Bias** prevents listeners from fully considering a position which opposes their own. Biases create significant problems for speakers and debaters. While we cannot change the pre-existing views and assumptions of our listeners, we may consider framing the argument using Socratic Design as the equivalent of entering a house through a side door rather than the front door. As listeners have a standing framework of attitudes and ideas about a topic, this forms something of a fortress which is difficult to breach. Ideally, we may bypass this fortress by entering through the side door. The listener is not prepared to engage and consider, rather only to defend. Catching listeners slightly off guard will ensure that their biases don't prevent them from considering a well-argued position.

Biases are responsible for listeners failing to pay full attention to a topic on which they already hold a position. For this reason, the traditional approach of beginning a persuasive argument with a premise, may be questioned and ultimately disregarded.

Review this list of controversial topics:

Safe Injection Sites

Decriminalizing Hard Drugs

Abortion

Gender Selection through Genetic Engineering

Religion's Role in Society Today

How much reading or research have you done on each of the topics above? Perhaps you have conducted some research on one of the particular topics of interest and perhaps none on other topics. Yet, it is very likely that you have a preformed opinion about each of these topics. Regardless of whether or not the opinion is an *educated* opinion, you will tend to be resistant to changing that opinion once it has been formed. This resistance is called **Confirmation Bias** or **Diagnosis Bias** and is a real psychological barrier to forming new opinions, even in the face of new evidence.

Further biases will be discussed in greater detail in the chapter entitled *Roadblocks: Biases, Heuristics, and Fallacies.*

Let's examine how bias may interfere from the outset in the persuasive process by comparing a traditional persuasive approach with the Socratic Design approach:

# Traditional Approach

Speaker: *Abortion is wrong and should be made illegal.*

Note that in this traditional approach, the speaker uses a declarative statement at the beginning or very early in the speech, to explicitly state her position.

Now, imagine yourself in the audience. Whether or not you have studied this issue, you likely hold a position.

Let's imagine first, that you are in *agreement* with this speaker. Studies have shown that you will most likely respond cognitively by affirming your own viewpoint (Lydon, Zanna, and Ross 1988; Petty and Cacioppo 1979; Chaiken 1980; Petty et al. 2004). In other words you will tell yourself something along these lines "That's right. I agree."

Remember that at this point, you haven't heard the speaker's full argument, just a statement of belief. Yet, you already align yourself with the speaker's viewpoint. This could be a mistake, which will be discussed in the chapter *Streetlight: The Mysterious Business of Changing Minds,* which discusses Social Judgment Theory. You believe that you already agree with the speaker and therefore, you have very little to no motivation to pay attention. We don't want to waste cognitive energy because thinking and processing require brain glucose. If expending energy is unnecessary, or offers little pay-off, we avoid it.

Therefore, you and half of the audience who also agree, stop listening.

Let's imagine now that you *disagree* with the speaker. What is the first thing that you do? Studies show that you are most likely to first resist the speaker's viewpoint by re-affirming your own view: *Yeah, well I bet she doesn't know any fourteen year olds who are pregnant and not ready to take care of a child.," etc.* The next thing you will do? Shut down completely. You will stop listening. You might even engage in a little defensive self-talk: *"Oh my goodness, I am so sick of these pro-lifers, I can't believe people think like this... etc."* What you definitely *don't* do, is to sit forward on your chair and listen intently so you can discover an alternative viewpoint. This is a problem. If we never encounter opposition arguments, we are not fully educated on a topic and we cannot make a fair, reasoned and educated decision.

Consequently, you and the other half of the audience who also disagree, stop listening.

So if those in agreement *and* those in disagreement have stopped listening, (even before the speaker gets to his or her first point) who *is* listening? No one. This is the primary reason that persuasion doesn't work. If we start with the wrong approach, we will fail. This should stand as common sense when we think about it as we are never persuaded by those who throw their opinions at us. It's not how persuasion works. Yet we regularly see persuasive speakers incorrectly format arguments using this informative structure.

The solution to the problem is simple: Re-frame the topic as a nonleading question:

*Should all abortion be legal?*

# Audience Engagement

© Anasta/Shutterstock.com

Although audience members still hold pre-existing views, the question-framing structure surprisingly changes the way that they perceive the discussion. If you don't know the speaker's position, you become curious. You listen to find out what the speaker believes. This strange phenomenon is called a *knowledge gap* and is explained by the Information Gap Theory of Curiosity (Loewenstein, 1994). Once we become aware that we don't know something, we suddenly want to know it, even if we didn't want to know beforehand. This is why we enjoy mysteries.

For example:

What city in the world is  most dangerous for a pizza delivery guy? Do you know the answer? Are you curious to know the answer? If you are like most people, now you want to know the answer, even though a few minutes ago you weren't even aware of the question.

Once we are aware of the gap in our knowledge, we thirst for the information.

Even if the knowledge gap doesn't work for every listener with regard to every topic, the question-framing approach will reduce the need for affirmation or defensive re-affirmation. Listeners are willing to pay attention to see what position you hold.

*The longer you keep your position a secret, the greater attention your audience will pay to your presentation.*

When a topic is framed as a *question* rather than a statement, audience engagement rises significantly. The audience becomes part of an active exploration process. They are curious and willing to pay attention as the argument unfolds before their eyes. They are active rather than passive participants. This makes a big difference on many levels: they don't tune out, they are cognitively engaged in examining and interpreting data, they are satisfying a human need to discover what they don't know (knowledge gap), and are likely to engage in critical thinking because they have a job to do (solving a problem).

Remember that in order for Socratic Design to be effective, you must not only refrain from giving away your position at the beginning of the speech, but also throughout most of the speech itself. Through Socratic questioning, you will lead the audience to *discover* your position. This discovery will take the form of additional questions and consideration of data on both sides of the argument. The specific structure will be outlined in the chapter entitled *Construction: A Fire Pentagon*.

Audience engagement is not just a "nice" thing to have when delivering a message; it is a crucial element in order to effect change. If people are not listening, they are not being impacted.

# Respect Autonomy

The final reason for using a Socratic Design is that it respects human beings' innate need for autonomy.

Humans place a high value on autonomy. Edward Deci identifies autonomy as one of three innate psychological needs (Deci 1987). Anything that challenges autonomy (or appears to do so) will be met with a degree of resistance. According to Psychological Reactance Theory, a person will respond with a degree of reactance when faced with a perceived threat to their personal freedom (S. Brehm and J. Brehm1981; Rosenberg and Siegel 2017). A study by Reich and Robertson (1979) showed that subjects were most resistant to messages with explicit commands.

The legal field reveres nonprejudicial argumentation and the use of nonleading questions is standard practice. According to the Federal Rule of Evidence, a question cannot suggest the answer to the person being questioned. The way questions are formed has been shown to have significant impact on resultant responses (Beckman 2014).

Most people can recall occasions where they felt that their autonomy was threatened, where they were perhaps being told what to do or what to think. As humans, we have a natural distaste for having ideas forced upon us; we wish to make our own choices.

The premise of Socratic Design is that we are asking the audience a nonleading question and will lead them through data to discover a conclusion. This model itself respects the autonomy of the human person because it gives them the freedom to choose *either* position, though we desire that they will choose the one which is in line with our viewpoint. The reason that this is possible lies within the structure itself. We will present the strongest data on both sides of the argument. The data alone should lead the audience to favor one position over the other.

A strong benefit to using this model is that once the audience discovers the conclusion themselves, they have a keen sense of ownership of this position, due to the fact that they have come to the conclusion on their own. The lasting value of response change is much more significant here than in cases where audiences have been told which position they should adopt.

# When to Use Conclusion Explicitness: The Exception

As noted above, with reference to advertising, the only case in which conclusion *explicitness* has been shown to be preferable to nonexplicitness is in direct marketing appeals. In other words, if you are a financial planner and you are inviting a friend to lunch in order to try to acquire his business, you should make your intentions clear from the outset. Do not surprise him with your pitch halfway through the meal, as he will not appreciate having what he thought to be a social event turned into a sales meeting. No one appreciates deceptive tactics.

# Does Persuasion equal Manipulation?

On the topic of deception, it is a common misconception that persuasion and manipulation are identical. This is false. Persuasion has the listeners'/consumers' best interests at heart, while in manipulation the speaker or salesperson has his own, rather than the audience's best interests at heart. Socratic Design prevents the use of manipulation due to the fact that it respects the freedom of the audience to choose a position, rather than having the speaker's view forced upon them.

---

**Everyday Conversation Practice**

1.  Use Socratic questioning any time there is discrepancy between you and your listener. Avoid the use of declarative statements such as "X is wrong, or Z is a bad idea." Instead, use question framing to engage. "Is X right or wrong? Or "Is Z a good or bad idea?" Note that the question always offers both options.

2.  Turn an uncomfortable discussion on a controversial topic into a Socratic conversation. By asking questions, you will engage your listener rather than making them defensive.

3.  Use Socratic questions when making a decision, even on a noncontroversial issue. Socratic questioning is the more effective method. Instead of stating "I don't want to go to that noisy restaurant" you can ask, "Should we go to the noisier restaurant or a quieter one?" This will help your partner to actively consider the sound levels of the restaurant. If you were hoping to have an important conversation over dinner, the answer should be obvious.

---

# EAST TO WEST: THE MYSTERIOUS BUSINESS OF CHANGING MINDS

Various theories have evolved to explain persuasion, where persuasion is defined as the changing of attitudes and their impact on future behaviors. Regardless of specific theoretical viewpoints, there is consensus on the concept of persuasion as *process* (Roskos-Ewoldsen 1997).

Imagine the persuasive process as follows:

?_____X

**Non-Leading Question**                    **Speaker's Viewpoint/Desired Conclusion**

Miller (1980, 2002) asserts that persuasion encompasses three distinct stages: response shaping, response reinforcement and response change. Response shaping refers to the initial contact with an object (message), while reinforcement refers to the strengthening or weakening of a pre-existing attitude regarding the object. Response change points to a shift in valence: positive or negative.

It is evident that some persuasive messages are accepted by particular audience members and rejected by others.

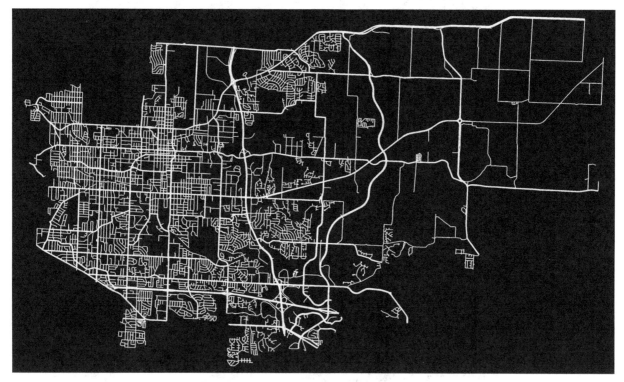

© ilyankou/Shutterstock.com

# Social Judgment Theory

Social Judgment Theory/Involvement Theory (Sherif, Sherif, and Nebergall 1965) investigates the role of pre-existing attitudes in perceived persuasiveness. This theory proposes three latitude zones which represent audience members' existing attitudes on a topic: **latitude of acceptance, latitude of rejection and latitude of noncommitment**. A latitude of acceptance is a range of positions which the listener finds acceptable at that particular moment in time. A latitude of rejection is a range of ideas that the audience finds unacceptable. A latitude of non-commitment is a range of ideas on which the audience does not hold a position and/or has never considered; this latitude lies somewhere between the latitudes of acceptance and rejection.

A listener's most accepted view on an issue is defined as his **anchor**. The anchor lies in the latitude of acceptance and will determine how attitudes embedded in the speaker's message will be received.

Inherent attitudes which lie in the audience's **latitude of rejection** are difficult if not impossible to change. Attitudes most likely to be affected by a message are those which lie in the latitudes of acceptance and noncommitment. While this is perhaps intuitive, there are two common errors in perception, one of which may be counter-intuitive. A message too far from a listener's anchor will be perceived to be further away ideologically than it actually is, and the listener will reject it with greater vigor. A message too close to the listener's anchor will be perceived to be closer than it actually is and the need for elaboration will be (erroneously) eliminated. In other words, a listener who believes that the speaker's message is too different from his own will fail to engage in central processing or elaboration and no persuasion will occur. Similarly, a listener who believes that the speaker's message is similar to, or the same as his own will believe that there is no need for analytical thought and reflection and will likewise fail to be persuaded (Sherif, Sherif, and Nebergall 1965).

This theory emphasizes that messages are not precise statements of the speaker's position, but are instead listener perceptions based on preformed ideas.

Social Judgment theory suggests that in choosing a persuasive topic, we should choose carefully. If the topic itself presents problems with speaker bias, we need to pay attention. There is no use in crafting a great message if the audience will refuse to engage with it to the degree that is necessary for change.

Let's look at an example of the use of the three latitudes of Social Judgment Theory:

**Topic**: What is the appropriate punishment for first-degree murder?

**Anchor**: Twenty-five-year jail sentence

(This is the listener's most accepted view and it is within the latitude of acceptance)

**Latitude of Acceptance**: Twenty-year jail sentence, life sentence

(Both of these options are acceptable options from the listener's perspective, one slightly more lenient and one slightly more harsh than the anchor)

**Latitude of Rejection**: Death penalty

(This is rejected as being too harsh)

**Latitude of Rejection**: Community rehabilitation

(This is rejected as being too lenient)

It is important to note here that latitudes of rejection will be on both sides of the latitude of acceptance. The latitudes of rejection as shown in the example, are on **opposite sides** of the latitude of acceptance, yet both are rejected as being too far, in one direction or another from the latitude of acceptance.

Between the latitude of acceptance and rejection (on both sides) are **latitudes of non-commitment.** These are positions which have neither been accepted nor rejected. They are perspectives which are either unfamiliar, or which have not been given sufficient thought or consideration.

For the topic of punishment, two latitudes of noncommitment may be as follows:

**Latitude of Noncommitment**: Twenty-year sentence without parole

(This Latitude of Noncommitment lies **between** Acceptance (twenty-five-year jail sentence) and Rejection (Death Penalty) on the more harsh side.

**Latitude of Noncommitment:** Fifteen-year sentence with mandatory weekly rehabilitation program attendance.

(This Latitude of Noncommitment lies **between** Acceptance (twenty-five-year jail sentence) and Rejection (Community Rehab) on the more lenient side.

***Social Judgment theory tells us that we should choose a perspective ("X" in the diagram) which lies in our audience's latitude of noncommitment.***

Because listeners have not given great consideration to this perspective, it is a speaker's best chance to minimize the significant concerns with pre-existing views. Choosing a topic or perspective within an audience latitude of noncommitment is the secret to skirting problems of bias and resistance. If an audience has not previously considered a particular angle on an issue or never been presented with a particular creative solution, they are much more likely to both engage while listening as well as to practice cognitive elaboration in the future.

?_____X

**Nonleading Question**                                    **Latitude of Non-C**

© Bubushonok/Shutterstock.com

# Human Motivation

When choosing X (or the conclusion you wish your audience to reach at the end of your message) consider what factors are at play in human motivation.

While you may have heard that people are motivated by money, love, lust, or power, all of these motivations may be categorized as motivations of **self-interest.** In popular discussion, some may argue that as human beings, our *only* interest is self-interest. Yet consider this: If you were walking on a deserted street and found a wallet lying on the ground in front of you, in an area without CCTV cameras, would you steal the wallet or would you turn it in?

While some people may choose to steal the wallet, others would not. If you said that you would turn in the wallet, the question is why? If you were only ever motivated by self-interest, then you would always steal the wallet, especially because without cameras in place there is little chance of being caught. There is clearly something else at play. When asked why you would turn in the wallet, as opposed to keeping it, you might respond that the wallet does not belong to you and that you consider yourself to be an honest person. Honest people don't steal things that don't belong to them. In this example, you are *identifying* yourself as an honest person.

The second human motivation, other than self-interest, is **identity**. Identity might be moralistic, gender-based, ethnic, religious, associated with a particular group, career, or hobby, etc. Identity is a powerful motivator. You may post something on social media that decries racism because you consider yourself to be (identify as) a fair and equitable person. You may make certain choices because you identify with a particular nationality: *Canadians are expected to be tolerant.* You may avoid certain behaviors because they conflict with the identity you have created for yourself: *Musicians never download music without paying for it.*

Remember that self-interest and identity do not only apply to choices we make within our own personal lives, but also reflect perspectives we adopt on a broad scale.

For example, if you consider yourself to be very forgiving person (identity) you will subconsciously be aware of how forgiving people are expected to behave. This will influence your views on topics, whether they relate back to you on a personal level or not. You may be more likely to accept the position *fifteen years with mandatory rehab* than the position *life without parole*. In other words, you are more likely to accept latitudes of commitment on one side of rejection than on the other side.

As you choose a persuasive objective (X), be sure that you carefully consider human motivations. How does your objective relate to either the audience's potential self-interest or to their identity? Be sure to appeal to either specific self-interest, specific identity, or appeal to both.


?_____X

**Nonleading Question**                                    **Latitude of NC Motivation**

---

### Everyday Conversation Practice

1. Try implementing Social Judgment Theory in daily conversation. When having a conversation on a touchy topic, try approaching it using your listener's latitude of noncommitment. This usually requires first listening to discover their latitudes of acceptance and rejection and then identifying an appropriate latitude of noncommitment.

1. Practice identifying your listener's motivation when attempting to exert influence. How do they see themselves (identity) and how can you appeal to that identity? What self-interest factors have the possibility to affect their viewpoint in order to change their behavior?

# STREETLIGHT:
## ILLUMINATING THINKING AND DECISION-MAKING

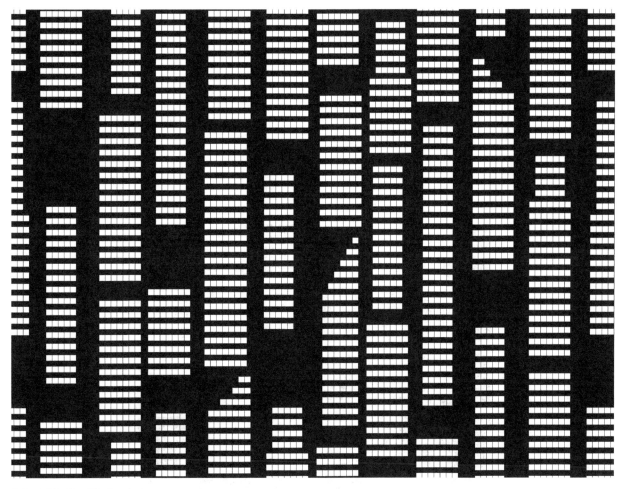

© Andy Vinnikov/Shutterstock.com

For the speaker who wishes to exert influence, knowledge and understanding of human thinking is essential. In particular, it is important to review the building blocks of thinking, due to the significant role that pre-existing attitudes play in the persuasive process. We will also examine the theories which cast light on the most effective way to design persuasive messages.

# The Building Blocks

In order to understand the factors at play in persuasion, let's examine the role of attitudes, beliefs, values and knowledge.

**Attitudes**: Likes or dislikes

Examples: You like hip hop music; dislike brussel sprouts; prefer dark beer over light

**Beliefs**: Something you hold to be true or false; an area of uncertainty. You believe something when you cannot know definitively whether or not it is true.

When you possess certainty that something is true, the idea no longer falls under the belief category, but the knowledge category.

Examples: Ghosts exist. UFOs do not exist.

**Values**: Concepts of right and wrong; good and bad

Examples: It is good to be honest; it is better to treat people fairly than unfairly

**Knowledge**: What we already know to be true

Examples: 2 + 2 = 4; Mars is a planet; milk is a liquid

© BEAUTY LIVES IN THE HEART/Shutterstock.com

It is helpful to know that attitudes are the easiest to change because they are superficial and may be changed with the introduction of a new experience. For example, you may not think that you like calamari, but if you take a bite of your friend's calamari at lunch and decide that it's not as chewy as you expected and you don't mind it, the new experience has shifted your attitudes. Beliefs are more difficult to change because they are more deeply rooted than attitudes and values are the hardest to change because they are so deeply rooted in us that we don't often recognize them until we need to make a decision (S. A. Beebe and S. J. Beebe 2018).

Consider whether your objective is to influence your audience's attitudes, beliefs, or values.

Although not every persuasive appeal is attempting to influence values, at the root of every controversial topic is a **value conflict.**

At the heart of the oil sands debate is a value conflict. While it is easy to get caught up in the details of the discussion—tailing ponds, dead birds, indigenous lands, job loss, fiscal futures—at the very heart of the debate, two values are at war. In this case the two values are the environment and the economy. Clearly both of these values are positive and we value each of them. In this context, however, we prioritize one value over the other, depending on our position. If you are on the environmental side, you will prioritize the environment over the economy. If you are on the opposite side of the debate, you will prioritize the economy over the environment. This is called a **value priority.**

Remember that value priorities are context-specific. In a different context, the same individual may prioritize a different value.

As persuasive speakers, we need to identify the value conflict and the value priority. Throughout the argument we should gradually reveal, through the data itself, which value deserves priority. This value should be justified within the specific context.

For example, toward the end of the speech we may either imply or state that while both values are important, the value which aligns with our position (X) is *more* important in this particular context.

# Behavioral Intention

Even if audience attitude (attitude/belief/value) change is successfully achieved, this may or may not result in a change in behavior. The gap between attitude acceptance and behavior change is bridged by what Ajzen and Fishbein (1975) called behavioral intention. This theory posits that behavioral intention is a better guide to behavior than attitude alone, as intention incorporates and accounts for the subjective norm. For example, Bob may have a favorable attitude toward getting a military-style haircut, but if his friends ridicule him for the idea, he may not get the haircut after all. This theory considers situational factors which may affect a person's future behavior.

While Susan may desire to visit Spain (favorable attitude), she may be prohibited from doing so due to her financial situation. Her lack of ability constrains her behavior, but her behavioral intention reflects her actual attitudes. In this case, behavioral intention is a more accurate indicator of attitude change than behavior itself. In the Theory of Planned Behavior, an adaptation of Reasoned Action Theory, volitional control is proposed to be significant to behavioral outcomes. (Ajzen, 1991).

Facts, opinions, assumptions, and inferences are the basic building blocks of arguments. It is crucial, as a speaker to understand the differences between them and the implications of these differences for implementation in an argument.

© BorisGodunov/Shutterstock.com

# Fact

The general consensus on defining a fact is that it can be proven **by evidence**.

*The state of Oregon lies on the west coast of the United States.*

Although this *definition* is not debated, there is a significant amount of discrepancy as to what is a fact and what is not a fact.

For example:

> *For the most part, men are physically stronger than women.*
>
> Is that a fact or an opinion?
>
> *The Bible is the inspired Word of God.*
>
> Fact or opinion?

While we think we can easily tell the difference between facts and opinions, in practice, it is not so easy. You may notice already that discrepancy as to whether these statements are fact or opinion will immediately affect any argument built upon such premises. If you think that something is a fact, but your audience sees it as opinion, you have a problem. Many arguments fail at this most basic level; they fail before they begin. It is essential that both you and your audience agree on such foundational elements. You may need to explain the fact/opinion difference and prove your point before asserting a fact as a fact.

Another interesting idea to peruse is how and when we accept something as a fact. Clearly, you have never seen Mars with your own eyes, yet you accept external evidence in order to believe it to be true. You have never met Socrates, yet you likely believe the stories as evidence that he was a real person.

Why do we accept some evidence at face value and not other evidence? It is a question to ponder.

# Opinion

Opinions are subjective personal views. Contrary to popular knowledge, there are two very distinct kinds of opinions and the difference between them is a crucial one.

An opinion that remains an opinion is called a **wavy-line opinion.**

For example: "*This carpet is ugly*" is an opinion. Someone else's opinion on the carpet may be different, as they may find the carpet attractive. In this case, neither person is correct or incorrect in their view, as the matter is subjective. There is no right or wrong answer.

However, let's look at this example: "*Ghosts exist.*"

While everyone is free to share their opinion on whether or not this statement is true or false, this is a very different kind of opinion. Is there a correct answer to this question?

Many people will answer "no" because it seems to be a simple matter of opinion. But wait.

Let's stop for a moment and review the definition of belief. A belief is a type of opinion. Beliefs are an area of uncertainty. The reason we don't know the answer of whether or not ghosts actually exist for sure is because collectively, as a society, we cannot agree that there is enough evidence to move "the existence of ghosts" from the belief bucket to the knowledge bucket. Note: You may have enough evidence yourself, to think that you know, rather than believe, however as a society, we cannot agree that sufficient evidence exists.

Just because we cannot agree, does it mean that there is no right answer to the question?

At this moment in time, we are expressing a subjective opinion, but, objectively speaking *there must be a correct answer to the question "Do ghosts exist?".* Why? Because the only logical options are yes, they exist and no, they do not exist. Logically, there are no other possibilities. So, there must be a correct answer, (either yes or no) even though *at this moment in time we do not know the answer.*

This kind of opinion is called a **straight-line opinion**: It begins as a subjective opinion, but ends in a fact.

Something else to consider is the idea that our personal wishes and desires have no influence on whether or not something does or does not exist.

Shane may wish for there to be intelligent life on other planets, but regardless of his desires, intelligent life either does or does not exist on other planets. Period.

Keeping subjectivity in check, particularly where it does not belong, is important. Kerri may exercise her right to think that 2 + 2 is 17, but her opinion becomes secondary, per se, in the face of fact. It cannot change reality. She has the right to have and share her opinion, but sometimes, opinions are wrong.

Let's look at some popular opinion discussions to determine the category to which they belong, wavy or straight-line opinions.

> **Political debate:** wavy-line opinion.
>
> Whether or not a party or candidate is doing a good job or a poor job, is a matter of subjective opinion. It is impossible to argue absolutes, correctness or incorrectness.
>
> **The UFO debate**: straight-line opinion.
>
> UFOs are either real or not. Period.
>
> **Vaccines should be mandatory debate:** wavy-line opinion.
>
> There is no correct or incorrect answer. It can be argued from a subjective perspective based on either a collective health safety perspective or an autonomy perspective.
>
> **Prisoners should have the right to vote debate**: wavy-line opinion.
>
> There is no correct answer. It is just an opinion.
>
> **God exists debate:** straight-line opinion.
>
> This is either true or not true. There are no other options. You may debate about what God is like or not like etc., but the *existence* of God question is a straight-line opinion. There is a correct answer and an incorrect answer. There either is a God or there is not a God.

Knowing that a question has a correct answer (even though we may never know the answer definitively in our own lifetime) does not mean that we can argue with arrogance, rather that we can gently remind our opponent that there *is* a correct answer. This should change the way we argue. If we know that a correct answer exists, the intelligent thing to do is not to persist in our own opinions, but to search for the truth.

# Problem of Noncontradiction

This means that two *logically opposing* ideas cannot both be true. Ghosts cannot exist *and* not exist. When one is true, the other must be false. This principle is often challenged based on examples such as: "*Roger can be both in and out of the room at the same time.*" This statement is logically untrue, but by Roger simultaneously standing with one foot in the room and the other foot outside of the room, it appears to be true, when really it is just a matter of playing with semantics. By changing the wording to "*Roger cannot be both fully inside the room and fully outside the room at the same time,*" the issue is no longer debatable and the principle stands.

# Assumption

An assumption is an idea which we believe to be true, without having seen supporting evidence.

Example:

> You park your car in the same lot every time you go to work. Do you believe that it will be there today when you go to get it? Likely you do. This is an assumption, because unless you have gone to check on your car, you really have no evidence that it is still in the lot. You base your belief on past experiences of your car being there at the end of the day, but, could you be wrong this time? Yes.

There is a saying which states "*when you assume, you make an 'ass' out of you ("u") and "me*". It's catchy, but it's mostly inaccurate. We make assumptions all day long. We have to do so to survive, because if we had to see evidence for everything in order to believe something to be true, we would never get out of bed. When you get up in the morning, do you know the floor is going to be there? No. However, you assume it will be there, as it has been every other morning. Assumptions are necessary.

What we do want to *avoid* is making unnecessary assumptions.

If your boss assumes that you are lazy because you were late for work this morning, this is an unnecessary (and unhealthy) assumption. There is no reason for him to make such an assumption, especially if you are usually on time for work. Unnecessary assumptions are the ones which get us into trouble and which we should carefully avoid.

# Inference

An inference is a specific assumption based on a more broad assumption. For example, if you believe that all lawyers make good money (a broad assumption) you may also then infer (smaller assumption) that if you become a lawyer that you also will make good money. As you can see here, if the broad assumption is incorrect, the inference will also be incorrect.

# Belief Immunodeficiency

While the aforementioned theories would assert unbelief as a default, Spinoza's Theory asserts belief as default. This theory suggests that the "belief reaction" is automatic and lasts for a minimum of a hundred milliseconds. At that point, the listener will process the information analytically, or via the neocortex, unless distracted. Through simple mental distraction, an individual may fail to engage in the analytical processing and essentially forget to unbelieve (Carpenter 2017).

Essentially, the theory posits that our default is to believe rather than not believe and if we fail to critically question the idea in time, we will forget to unbelieve it.

For example, if a friend tells you, "*There is a rabbit in New Zealand which is called Lapis Lux*," you would likely believe her. There is no reason for you *not* to believe what she has just said. Your default is to believe. Now, in the next hundred milliseconds after hearing this information, even if you were skeptical of it in the first place, if in that brief period you are *distracted by something else, y*ou will forget to even question this fact. Three months later you might tell another friend about this rabbit in New Zealand, which in this case, of course, does not really exist. Distraction after learning a new fact is the key to belief immunodeficiency. It may be a good idea to keep an eye on certain politicians, when they state a "fact" and then quickly follow that fact with a shocking or concerning statement. We tend to focus immediately on this latter distraction, while the first "fact" goes mentally unchecked and recalled later as truth.

Kevin Dutton (2011) tells a true story about belief immunodeficiency, in his book *Split-Second Persuasion.* A couple in Scotland had rented a hotel in the countryside for a wedding reception. The best man was in charge of keeping an eye on the wedding gifts and had been checking on them intermittently throughout the evening, on a table in the front lobby. On one of these occasions when he went to check on the gifts, they were gone. He asked the receptionist where she had put the gifts. The receptionist replied that "the men in the truck had come to take them to the house." Since the couple lived 700 miles away, the groom had no idea what she was talking about. There was no house and there had been no arrangement to move the gifts. When the receptionist realized what had happened, she broke down in tears. Earlier in the evening, a truck had pulled up and some men in uniforms had gotten out and said they were there to move the gifts. She said that she had had no reason to disbelieve them, as they looked the part. Now, at the very same time that these men had entered the building, the receptionist had been *distracted* by the guest in room 308 who was asking about his room service. This timely distraction prevented the receptionist from second-guessing their intentions and she did not bother to ask them for ID. They took the gifts and left. The man in room 308 turned out to be an accomplice.

Her initial and *default instinct* was to believe that the movers were who they claimed to be, and the moment of *distraction* prevented her from questioning that initial belief.

While belief immunodeficiency can be exploited by con artists, it can also be used in a legitimate way by ethical speakers. Ethical use of the technique means that there is no deceit or manipulation involved---that the speaker is not using the technique to do any harm to the listener.

# Three Theories

We will examine three theories of thinking/decision-making and then discuss in detail, in the chapter entitled *Construction: A Fire Pentagon,* why and how knowledge of these theories is a gold mine for the persuasive speaker.

These theories are called dual process theories; they seek to explain how humans think, learn and make decisions. Dual process theories identify two routes to persuasion. Early theorists established the idea that there are two distinct processes of thought, a central, or consciously cognitive process and an unconscious or peripheral route (James 1884). Richard Petty and John Cacioppo (1986) call these routes central processing and peripheral processing. Central route processing involves active cognitive participation by the listener. Peripheral processing occurs when focus is on peripheral cues such as speaker attractiveness rather than on message substance. An audience member who analyzes the pros and cons of political arguments presented is using cognitive processing, whereas an audience member who develops a favorable attitude toward the candidate based on the latter's physical attractiveness is using peripheral processing in decision-making (Gass and Seiter 2011).

# Systems 1 and 2

In Tversky and Kahneman's Systems 1 and 2 dual process theory (1981), System 2 is the slower, more deliberate and analytical cognitive system, while System 1 is the faster, intuitive emotional system. While System 2 has often been perceived to be the "leader" in earlier dual process theories, Kahneman suggests that this is false and that System 1 is the default system, only requiring the assistance of System 2 when necessary. His research suggests that there is no evidence for simultaneous processing and that one system or the other is at work (Kahneman 2011). Evans and Stanovich (2013) also favor a model where System 1 decisions prevail as the default, unless higher-order (System 2) thinking intervenes.

Chip and Dan Heath (2011) refer to System 1 as the Elephant and System 2 as the Rider.

As the default system, the elephant has the greater control.

## Elaboration Likelihood Model

**Elaboration Likelihood Model** (ELM) (Petty and Cacciopo 1986) places primary focus on pre-existing audience attitudes in shaping a message, while Cognitive Dissonance Theory argues that persuasion itself is a reactive response to restoring equilibrium when attitudes or beliefs are challenged (Festinger 1957).

The ELM suggests that central processing requires cognitive elaboration, which entails mental engagement with message content. Elaboration occurs on a continuum, with maximum elaboration at one end of the continuum and no elaboration on the opposite end (Petty and Cacioppo 1986; Petty 2017). While Petty and Cacioppo acknowledge that simultaneous processing may occur, there is a tendency for individuals to favor one route over the other. An individual with high issue involvement coupled with the ability to pay attention and comprehend the message will likely use central processing whereas an individual with low issue involvement may use peripheral processing. While research shows that listener attitudes may be changed via either route, central route processing may be more desirable because attitude effects are longer-lasting (Petty, Haugtvedt, and Smith 1995).

# Heuristic Systematic Model

Similarly, the **Heuristic Systematic Model** (Chaiken 1980) posits that systematic processing requires listener motivation and ability. One distinction of the HSM is the sufficiency principle, which suggests that listeners desire to receive a sufficient amount of information to reach a decision, neither more, nor less. The two systems work together to find the correct balance.

Notably, if a speaker can reduce initial bias he will increase engagement, which in turn will increase likelihood of elaboration.

In further chapters, we will examine how to frame data in order to ensure that our listeners are using System 1 when System 1 thinking is required, how to ensure System 2 is engaged at the right moment, but not too early and how to manage data to deliver the right amount of data for maximum results.

---

### Everyday Conversation Practice

1. Think about your own opinions and determine which opinions are wavy-line opinions and which are actually straight-line opinions.

2. Think about a topic you have heard discussed in the media. Jot down what you believe to be true. Review your list and identify which of those are facts, which are opinions and which are assumptions. You may be surprised.

3. Try using belief immunodeficiency in an ethical manner, in an everyday conversation. Deliver a fact and then distract your listener with another fact immediately afterward. Ethical use means that there is no manipulation or deceit involved.

4. Begin to identify straight-line opinions in everyday debates. Help your listener to see that not all opinions are of the same type and that this should affect the way the debate evolves.

# ROADBLOCKS:
# BIASES, HEURISTICS AND FALLACIES

© Dmitriip/Shutterstock.com

?_____0_____0_0_____X

Even the best arguments may be met with resistance, as humans have been shown to be cognitively predisposed to resist attempts at persuasion.

Roadblocks come in many forms. Anything that stops an audience from listening is problematic. It is advisable to be aware of the potential problems that may arise and to do everything possible to avoid or mitigate them.

Fransen, Smit, and Verlegh (2015) identify four overarching categories of resistance: avoidance strategies, empowerment strategies, contesting strategies and biased processing strategies.

# Avoidance Strategies

Avoidance strategies are passive strategies in which the listener attempts to avoid the message. With cognitive avoidance, a listener may tune out a speaker whose viewpoint differs from his own. This is a significant obstacle in persuasion, as it precludes a listener from processing even the best of arguments. As mentioned earlier, humans place a high value on autonomy. Numerous studies (Buller et al. 2000; Dillard and Shen 2005) confirm the negative impact of assertive language and commands, pointing to the assertion that they have a boomerang effect, wherein the recipient is more entrenched in his own position.

# Empowerment Strategies

Empowerment Strategies work to reinforce existing attitudes by actively reviewing data which reinforce those views, rather than considering opposition arguments on the basis of their merits (Lydon, Zanna, and Ross 1988; Petty and Cacioppo 1979; Chaiken 1980; Petty, Tormala, and Rucker 2004). Skepticism is an inclination toward disbelief. In a persuasive speech, for example, a listener may be skeptical toward the speaker, his credentials or intentions, the validity of data presented and the value of the message (Petty and Cacioppo 1979; Chaiken 1980; Petty, Tormala, and Rucker 2004).

# Contesting Strategies

Contesting strategies are active strategies where the listener responds with counterarguments. The message is considered in the context of a listener's existing issue-relevant attitudes and beliefs instead of being given objective consideration. Active cognitive participation is required to formulate oppositional responses. Counterarguments may be heightened when explicit persuasive intent is revealed to listeners (Niederdeppe et al. 2012).

A Socratic message design, using the latitude of noncommitment, drastically reduces if not eliminates the likelihood of listeners using avoidance, empowerment and contesting strategies.

Biased processing requires additional cautions on the part of the speaker.

*Biases refer to subconscious attitudes while fallacies refer to the poor use of logical reasoning within an argument. Often times, fallacies are rooted in biases.*

# Biased Processing Strategies

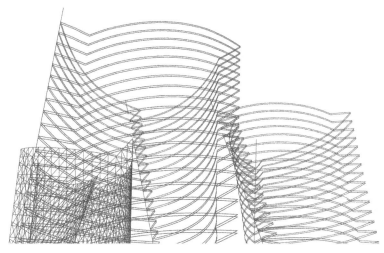

© Yurii Andreichyn/Shutterstock.com

Biased processing refers to the power of pre-existing attitudes. Since humans are a product of their past experiences and knowledge, it is easy for us to allow past encounters to shape our view of future events or of people we have never met.

Malcolm Gladwell's book *Talking to Strangers* addresses bias as a systemic problem and one that is not easy to fix because of its deep-rooted and far-reaching effects. He shows how many societal biases are rooted in earlier biases which have failed to be addressed therefore causing systematic dysfunction. Gladwell illustrates this with the story of a black woman who was pulled over for a simple traffic violation by a white police officer. When the officer forces her to exit the vehicle, the encounter escalates into an ugly scene. The woman is arrested and sent to jail. Since she was new in town and had just accepted a career position at a university, the shame of being sent to jail caused the woman to despair, which ended in her suicide. The reason that the woman was pulled over in the first place was problematic. The police officer was following an outdated protocol which was completely irrelevant and unnecessary. The protocol had been implemented hundreds of miles away, a few years earlier and required officers to be aware of black individuals looking suspicious in one specific neighborhood, again, miles away from where this incident occurred. The concern of racial profiling here alone should be a red flag, but beyond that, there is another concern. The protocol that the officer was using made no sense in the context in which it was being used. This is an example of an earlier bias leading to a new bias leading to a further bias.

Anything that causes you to see a new situation or an unfamiliar individual through the lens of your past experiences is a bias. Biases can be both negative and positive, but it is the negative biases which are most concerning. A social worker, let's call her Darla, may deal with many unfit parents in her career, but if Darla automatically assumes the guilt of a parent whom she is meeting for the first time, prior to conducting a fair investigation, this negative bias may lead Darla to reach an erroneous conclusion because she will view the parent through the lens of her own past experiences. It is evident that some biases can have very serious consequences.

**Heuristic processing** refers to processing which bypasses deliberate, critical thought (Kahneman's System 2 thinking) and relies on System 1 thinking which is quick, intuitive and emotional (Tversky and Kahneman1974; Kahneman 2011). While System 1 has legitimate function, it does not involve assessment of the merits and weakness of logical arguments. When System 1 is used to process data, it reverts to mental shortcuts and inaccurate conclusions may be drawn. For example: *John is an introvert, who wears glasses and loves to read. Is John more likely to be a farmer or a librarian?* Many people may conclude that John is more likely to be a librarian—a conclusion reached by referencing mental schemas regarding librarians. The tendency to focus on the glasses and the reading details lead the listener to an erroneous conclusion. The question asks if John is more *likely* to be a farmer or librarian. Statistically, there are more male farmers than librarians, so John is actually more likely to be a farmer. This is called the **Focusing Illusion.** The one committing this heuristic thinking is focusing too much on the glasses and books and too little on the word "likely."

The reason that heuristic thinking is so common is because System 1 is our default system. Unless we deliberately engage our critical thinking system, we will use these mental shortcuts in decision-making. Awareness of our natural tendencies can help us avoid heuristic thinking and help us strategize to help our audiences avoid the same mistakes.

**Confirmation Bias or Diagnosis Bias** is the heuristic bias of processing information in such a way that it conforms to existing attitudes (Wason and Johnson-Laird 1972). A study which examined whether or not adults change their minds after reading persuasive text concluded that adults do not weigh arguments mindfully, considering evidence in order to make a decision, instead they pay attention only to data which reinforce preexisting beliefs (Chambliss and Garner 1996). While this study approached the question of persuasive effectiveness based on written text, modality does not seem to be a factor when studying cognitive biases, therefore the results may be considered for oral persuasion as well.

**Availability Bias** is the mental shortcut of making a decision based on information that is readily available. For example, if you are asked: *Which is more common, death by flood or death by asthma,* you would quickly search your memory for examples of each. Death by floods? Yes! You can easily recall hearing about villages that were flooded and many people losing their lives. You may think of numerous examples. Now, death by asthma? This time, when you search your memory, you come up with nothing. You know asthma can be serious but you don't remember hearing about anyone dying from it. Therefore, you quickly reach the conclusion that death by floods is more common but you would be incorrect. Death by asthma is much more common. The reason that you came to the wrong conclusion is because the information you accessed was the information which was readily available to you. Where did you hear about death from floods? Likely from watching or reading the news. Floods are more sensational than breathing difficulties and therefore what makes the news and what doesn't make the news can bias our perceptions of reality.

**Fundamental Attribution Error.** If you have ever driven on a busy road, you might understand this error. Can you recall a time when you were driving, going the speed limit and a driver approaches from your right, races by you and cuts in front? Sound familiar? What was your response? For many people, the word "jerk" comes to mind or something less flattering. You think the other driver is a jerk for speeding and for cutting you off. Now, be honest. Have *you* ever been the other guy, speeding and cutting someone off? If so, you're not alone. Are *you* a jerk? Of course not! Why not? Because the reason that you were driving this way is because you were in a hurry, right? You had to get to an important interview! You explain your own behavior by referring to context, whereas you explain the other's behavior as being related to his character. This is fundamental attribution error.

**Halo Effect** is the tendency to attribute positive qualities to someone based on other qualities which they possess. For example, let's say you have met your neighbor Joe only one time. He seemed friendly and he seems like a neat person as he keeps his yard nicely trimmed. These qualities of friendliness and neatness are seen as positive qualities. Therefore, if someone asks you if Joe is honest, when using the halo effect, you will likely assume that he is indeed honest. Why? Because Joe is friendly and neat, you are likely to attribute other positive qualities to him automatically and of course, irrationally.

# Fallacies

Fallacies are logical arguments that are based on unsound reasoning.

We want to ensure that we avoid using fallacies in our own arguments. In addition, we may identify them in other arguments so that we do not make irrational decisions based on poor logic.

## Ad Hominem Abusive

Attacking the person rather than the idea.

Example:

A politician calling an opponent "ugly."

## Ad Hominem Circumstantial

Disregarding a source due to their "self-interest."

Example:

A voter disregarding a military officer's push for increased funding to the military because the military officer has self-interest.

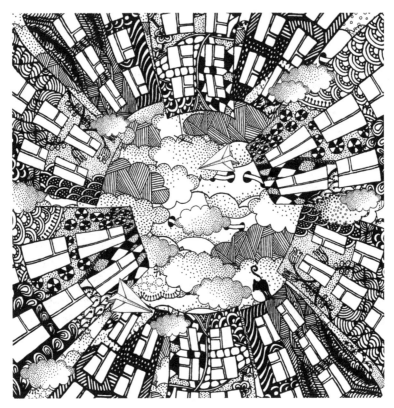

© ImHope/Shutterstock.com

# Genetic Fallacy

Disregarding an argument due to its source.

Example:

> Reading a study and automatically rejecting it because it was put out by the government.

In essence, the first three fallacies are considered to be under the umbrella of genetic fallacies because they promote or reject an idea based on the source rather than on the merit of the argument itself.

# Mob Appeal

Arguing that we should do something because everyone else is doing it.

Example:

> Everyone drinks beer, so you should too.

# Snob Appeal

Arguing that we should not do something because everyone else is doing it. An appeal to elitism.

Example:

*A truck ad which states: "This truck is for real men."*

## Appeal to Illegitimate Authority:

Using an individual as a source when they do not possess credibility on the topic.

Example:

A celebrity using their fame to comment on issues on which they have no actual credibility.

## Chronological Snobbery

Appealing to something's age to justify either accepting or rejecting it.

Example:

This iPhone is the best because it is the newest version.

Example:

Roger's ideas are ridiculous because he is an old man.

## Irrelevant Goals or Functions

Assuming an incorrect goal or function of a practice or policy and therefore disregarding the practice or policy itself.

Example: A philosophy degree is useless because it won't pay the bills. (This may not be the individual's motivation for getting the degree; it may instead be to acquire reasoning skills or to be used as a stepping stone.)

## Irrelevant Thesis

Arguing something irrelevant to the case at hand.

Example:

America should outlaw gun ownership because my cousin shot himself in the foot with a gun.

## Straw Man

Attempting to disprove an opponent's beliefs by presenting them in an inaccurate light.

This may be deliberate or accidental.

Example:

> I heard that Catholics worship the Virgin Mary.

# Begging the Question (Circular Reasoning)

Answering a question by simply re-wording the question as an answer. Aka saying nothing of value.

Example:

> We are in an economic recession because we have seen a downturn in the financial sector.

# Bifurcation

Framing a debate so that only two options exist. (There are almost always more than two potential options.)

Example:

> The current justice system is not working so we need the death penalty.

Of note, this fallacy can be subtle. It is easy to get taken by such arguments because if we agree that the current system is not working, then we may think that the other option is the logical alternative. Unfortunately, this is not accurate as there are many options in between the two options presented.

# Fallacy of Moderation

Arguing that the truth is always "in the middle."

Example:

> The truth is always in the middle.

Sometimes the truth *is* in the middle, but the fallacy is assuming that this is always the case.

# Is-Ought Fallacy

Assuming that because something is a certain way, that it ought to be that way.

Example:

> Divorce is inevitable, as we have a high divorce rate in America.

# Division

Parts of a whole will have all the characteristics of the whole.

Example:

My steak will taste just like the steaks at Ace Steak House if I use their seasoning salt sold at the grocery store.

# Composition

The whole will share all characteristics of the individual pieces.

Example:

Harvard is a school full of geniuses.

# Hasty Generalization

Reaching a conclusion on the basis of too few examples.

Example:

All 25 year old guys are bad drivers.

# Sweeping Generalization

Taking a generalization which is perhaps largely true and failing to acknowledge that exceptions could exist.

Example:

All men deserve freedom. (Largely true, except that those who are imprisoned lose some of their freedoms.)

# False Analogy

Attempting to draw an analogy between two things not similar enough to warrant the analogy.

Example:

Don't eat turkey for Thanksgiving, because we shouldn't eat animals. You wouldn't eat your dog, would you?

# False Cause

Using a weak connection in an attempt to prove causation.

Example:

> Every time I win a marathon it's because I am carrying my lucky rabbit's foot in my pocket.

# False Precision

Using numbers in too precise a way to be justified.

> Example:There have been 121,014 wars in the course of history.

(It's not possible to know the exact number. In this case it is better to suggest approximation than precision. )

# Equivocation

An argument which is built around ambiguous language.

Example:

> Murder is wrong.

The ambiguous language is problematic because your definition may differ significantly from your audience's definition of what constitutes murder.

# Accent

Placing improper or deceptive emphasis on particular words or phrases.

Example:

> This orange juice is organic.

The word organic is being used very loosely here, to mean "natural" or without additives, but it can be deceiving as it implies that the juice is *certified organic,* which means that the juice has been produced according to very specific certification standards.

# Distinction without a Difference

Making a linguistic distinction between two things which are not, by nature, different.

Example:

> My son is not a bully! He just likes to beat up smaller kids.

# Meta-Intolerance

Intolerance of intolerance. Using intolerance itself as a reason to disregard a viewpoint.

Example:

   They are wrong because they are intolerant.

Intolerance itself is not a valid argument. By saying they are wrong because they are intolerant is being intolerant of intolerance. Find a specific, concrete reason rather than claiming intolerance.

# Cognitive Overload

While cognitive overload is neither a bias nor a fallacy, it is a significant obstacle in the persuasion process. Cognitive load theory explains that information overload occurs when attentional resources have reached maximum capacity and cognitive resources required for understanding and retention are no longer available. For example, a speaker overwhelmed with existing concerns (high extraneous load) and then overwhelmed with new hard data such as facts and statistics (high intrinsic load) will not have the resources to associate that data into schemas (germane load), and will fail to assimilate and recall the information (Chandler and Sweller 1991; Paas, Van Gog, and Sweller 2010).

© cepera/Shutterstock.com

# How to Overcome/Mitigate Obstacles

Given the existence of potential obstacles to successful persuasion, it logically follows to investigate strategies to overcome or mitigate these obstacles.

Question framing of both the primary question and the use of subsequent question framing mitigates confrontation and defensive argumentation. Question framing can prevent confirmation bias and other biases based on pre-existing attitudes.

As mentioned earlier, the use of latitudes of noncommitment are also a strategic way to prevent the influence of pre-existing ideas.

Careful consideration in framing *data* appears to be an effective way to mitigate reactance and increase engagement. Framing is the way we present information. Every time we present data, we frame it in a particular way. The frame itself will affect the way the data is received.

Throughout the next few chapters we will discuss how to frame data in our messages for maximum impact.

---

**Everyday Conversation Practice**

1. Begin to take note of inherent biases and logical fallacies in everyday conversations. Once you look for them, you will likely be surprised at how common they are.

2. Avoid falling into the trap of buying into an idea, based on a mental shortcut. Fake news is everywhere. Become an intelligent consumer of ideas.

3. Consider the roadblocks that you may be using in your own arguments. Change your habits, starting with your everyday conversations and discussions.

---

# CONSTRUCTION:
## A FIRE PENTAGON

?_____X

NONLEADING QUESTION                                          LATITUDE OF NC

The Fire Pentagon structure synthesizes principles and theories informed by cognitive science, neuroscience and psychology. This framework is designed to maximize audience attention, ensure equitable examination of a question, retain audience engagement, facilitate critical thinking and encourage elaboration.

The pentagon is ordered that the speaker answers five questions during the preparation stage; the pentagon is then flipped to provide an ideal framework for delivery.

# Fire Pentagon
## Preparation

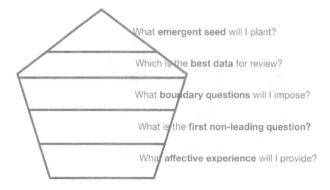

## Delivery

Let's look first at an overview of the process, then zoom in to examine the structure in greater detail.

# Overview

The process begins with the end in mind. While we may consider the first nonleading question to be the initial step in the process, it is important to realize that this question may change or be altered as you go through this process. At step 3, you will re-consider whether your initial leading question is the best leading question.

**Preliminary Step: Find the nonleading question (initial version)**

**Step 1: Identify the emergent seed.**

**What is the seed I wish to plant in my audience's mind at the end of my presentation?**

Due to the undisputed fact that persuasion is a process, rather than a single event, the speaker's objective should be to plant a seed in the minds of the listeners.

A persuasive appeal must leave the audience with something concrete—sometimes a call to action (based on a seed idea) and sometimes simply the seed itself which will take root in good time. The seed should be given careful thought and chosen according to its potential for exerting either immediate or gradual influence. The seed should be specific and concrete rather than vague and abstract. It should be a kernel that is so intriguing or mind-blowing that your audience won't be able to stop thinking about it. In order to facilitate recall, we will embed memory triggers within the message to help the audience remember the seed at the optimal time. The idea of planting a seed is based on Emergence Theory.

**Emergence Theory** has long been understood in the sciences, but has not been applied to human learning until recently. A chemist pouring one drop of a reagent at a time into a chemical solution may conclude that no reaction is taking place, because the solution appears to have remained unchanged. With the addition of a tenth drop, the solution suddenly bubbles and changes color. There is nothing significant about the tenth drop; the changes were occurring under the surface, yet invisible to the eye. The addition of the tenth drop was the catalyst which ignited the final change (Mighton 2008). The idea that small changes take place without being visible may explain why one day a child seems confused by the rules of reading and the next day is able to read complete sentences.

As emergence theory applies to human learning, it also applies to the understanding of new information in a persuasive message. We never know whether the seed we plant is the first "drop" in the solution or the final drop which causes change. Either way, it is our job to find the best possible seed to exert influence.

**Step 2: Identify best data on both sides of the argument**

Once you have identified this objective or end goal (X in the diagram above), the next step is to consider best data. **What is the *best* data to point to this conclusion (X)?**

Once you have determined what this data may be, you will also need to consider the best opposition data on the other side of the argument.

In order to respect the audience's autonomy to make their own decision, we will present the best data on both sides. This is the only way to fairly represent the issue. A message which slants the data toward a position by leaving out important but contradictory data is not an ethically designed message.

The way that we structure and present this data will be discussed in greater detail below.

**Step 3: Identify boundary questions.**

The next step is to determine your boundary questions. These questions will determine the parameters of your argument.

**Boundary questions** are questions which need to be answered in order to answer the primary (first nonleading) question. These questions set the boundaries for the argument. The goal is to allow the audience to explore freely, exerting their autonomy, but within constrained boundaries set by the speaker.

© doomu/Shutterstock.com

For example, if the primary or first nonleading question is: *Should tuition be reduced for online university classes,* consider what questions need to be answered in order to finally answer this question.

Depending on your audience's awareness level, (see chapter entitled *Kiosk: Sales Toolkit*) the boundary questions may look very different. Some potential boundary questions for this topic: *Can universities afford to decrease tuition? Will the quality of education also decrease, if tuition decreases? Is it the best choice? How much is enough to consider it to be an adequate decrease?*

Note that the boundary questions themselves should be controversial questions in order to faciliate a well-rounded discussion providing data from contradictory perspectives. These boundary questions also help retain the robust tension inherent in controversy which is desirable for maintaining audience engagement.

Non-controversial questions may be answered as data points within appropriate boundary questions. For example, you may wish to answer: Who has the final decision in reducing tuition? etc., Choose the *best* boundary questions for your objective, with your specific target audience in mind. Make sure that the boundaries you set are going to give your audience enough scope and content for exploration while still controlling the flow of data.

It should be noted here that the boundary questions you choose will determine the direction of the argument. Choose the boundary questions wisely.

**Step 4: Re-visit and tweak the initial nonleading question. Be sure that it is exactly the question you need to answer in order to lead your audience to X.**

At this juncture, re-visit your preliminary non-leading question to ensure that it is still the *best* question for this purpose. Remember that re-framing the question slightly can have significant effects on the remainder of the presentation. Oftentimes after discovering interesting or compelling data and identifying boundaries for the discussion, the initial question can be tweaked for maximum effectiveness. Frame the question to be engaging and specific, within the audience's latitudes of noncommitment.

**Step 5: Identify a visceral experience for the audience**

**Create a visceral experience for the audience.** Begin the speech by providing the audience with an **experience;** an experience in this context is defined as anything which provokes the audience to an **emotional response**. This emotional response may be positive or negative and it is the fire behind the momentum of persuasive argumentation.

This experience will be the hook at the beginning of your speech. A visceral experience makes the audience feel something at a gut level: Telling the audience that the Blendtec is a powerful blender is not a visceral experience; showing the Blendtec crush a Barbie doll is a visceral experience. Showing a PowerPoint slide on monthly spending is not a visceral experience; showing the audience a pile of products purchased in a month, complete with price tags, is a visceral experience.

**Remember to answer the questions in the order of the first pentagon in the preparation stage and *flip* the pentagon for delivery.**

The visceral experience will become the hook at the beginning of the speech while emergence will become the conclusion.

Now let's zoom in to examine details of the process and structure.

# Zooming In: How and Why

## Emergence and the Use of Memory Triggers

Cognitive neuroscientist Carmen Simon, author of Impossible to Ignore: Creating Memorable Content to Influence Decisions (2016) offers valuable insights into the use of memory triggers.

Human decision-making relies heavily on memory. Our memory is more useful prospectively than retrospectively. Prior knowledge and past experience inform our future choices. Because memory works by association, a speaker must make intentional choices to include memory triggers for the audience so that by association, listeners will recall the seed at the optimal time.

To find a memory trigger or triggers answer the following four questions:

1.  When do I need my audience to recall this seed?

2.  Where will they be at that time?

3.  What external triggers will be present in their environment?

4.  What internal mental triggers will help my audience with recall?

First consider the length of time between point A (the delivery of your message) and point B (when they need to recall the message). If the time between A and B is short (minutes to a few days) you can use **verbatim** memory triggers. If the length of time between points A and B is longer (days to months or years) use **gist** memory triggers.

Verbatim memory works with exact word for word recall, while gist memory delivers a big picture concept. People can recall exact wording only for short periods, but will remember big picture ideas longer. Your audience may recall "Vote Roy Webber" (verbatim trigger) for a few days if you repeat the slogan enough times at point A. However, if you want them to recall the idea in six months, it would be better to plant a gist trigger (Vote for the People's Party) because this broad idea will be easier to recall over time.

Simon gives an example of an effective external memory trigger. Nicorette, a gum product designed to help smokers kick the habit, advertises on packets of matches. Think about it. When do you want a smoker to think about quitting? When they are about to light a cigarette. What is already in their environment at that moment? Matches. External memory triggers are very helpful, but since you can't always predict a listener's future environment, plant internal memory triggers as well. An internal memory trigger might be " when you think about tax returns, think digital".

# Best Data

**Remember that scientific enquiry consists NOT of proving a hypothesis, but by attempting to disprove a null hypothesis. In investigating an idea, we should strive to disprove what we think we know or believe to be true. Only when we have done this, can we say that we have undertaken an intellectually honest enquiry.**

Answer each boundary question by examining the **best data on *both sides* of the argument**. Give fair representation to the arguments on the opposition side; don't be afraid of including compelling data. If your position is the more accurate, "better" position, the truth will emerge. It is important that you do not editorialize the data. *See how stupid this argument is,* or *So you can see how this proves my point.* Avoid this.

Instead, present the data and let it speak for itself.

For example:

> *"Those who support this position will point you to this study which says...* and *"the other side would argue that ..."* etc.

© ALEXOM11/Shutterstock.com

Avoid showing your hand. The audience should not be tipped to your position until at least 75 percent of the way through the presentation. This can be a challenging task, but it has been shown to be a worthwhile one.

Before discussing how to reveal your position at the 75 percent mark, let's look more closely at data architecture.

# Data Architecture: Logical Reasoning

Once you have discovered a fair representation of data on both sides of the argument, think carefully about how to arrange that data in order to lead the audience through a logical thinking process. We must be able to lead an audience to engage in critical thought, regardless of their current level of logical reasoning skills. Reasoning must become a framework for the data. Think of logical reasoning as a way to string the pieces of data together so the listener can understand the implications of that data.

Data should be presented and interpreted, without being editorialized.

Data alone is not convincing. The audience needs the data to be interpreted.

Here is the process:

1. Present the data

2. Interpret the data by answering the question: **What does this mean?**

3. Avoid editorializing by sharing your personal comments, feelings or perspectives, at least for the first 75% of the message.

**What does it mean** is a question that propels the argument forward by taking information (data) and putting it in a *context* within the conversation about your topic.

For example:

> *"Should masks be mandatory indoors?"*
>
> Imagine that the data on both sides is simply presented as stand alone data.
>
> (For)
>
> > A. The virus is airborne.
> >
> > B. Dr. Bob Smith says masks protect others from our droplets.
>
> (Against)
>
> > C. We have constitutional freedoms and mandatory masks do not respect those freedoms.
> >
> > D. There are only a few cases of the virus in our city.

Note that there are two pieces of "best" data on both sides of the argument. Without any data interpretation, the listener has to decide which side they find more compelling based on these simple statements. However, that would be an over-simplification. By asking "what does this mean" after each piece of data, we lead the audience to logically consider the *implications* of the data.

(For mandatory masks)

A.  "The virus is airborne." *What does this mean?* If data is airborne, this suggests that we need to look more carefully at how and when transmission is taking place. How long can aerosols remain in the air? Can enough micro-droplets remain in the air to infect a person who is not wearing a mask? How many people have gotten ill from inhaling droplets in a public place? Is it a small number or a larger number? You can see that sometimes the data leads to more questions, which is in fact what happens organically in scientific inquiry. Sometimes we can find data to answer the questions and other times the questions will remain for consideration. Don't force conclusions without adequate enquiry.

B.  "Dr. Bob Smith says that masks protect others from our droplets." *What does this mean?* It means that if my mask protects others and not myself, then my decision whether or not to wear a mask becomes a decision about other people etc.

*(Against mandatory masks)*

C.  "We have constitutional freedoms and mandatory masks do not respect those freedoms." *What does this mean?* This would suggest that those freedoms are more important than what the masks propose to protect us from... is this accurate? This might suggest that the government or someone wishes to restrict our freedoms. Is this accurate? Is it plausible? Is there other evidence to suggest this?

D.  "There are only a few cases of the virus in our city." *What does this mean?* It either means that the virus is not very contagious, that we have done a good job of preventing spread or that the virus is gone. What evidence can we find to support any of these ideas? Etc.

This process tells the story of the data in such a way that listeners are forced to engage in logical reasoning, rather than jumping to rash conclusions without considering implications. We can string the data/data interpretation together in a logical framework, using either causal reasoning, inductive reasoning, deductive reasoning or abductive reasoning.

# Causal Reasoning

Causal reasoning suggests a causal relationship between two things. A causes B.

Causal reasoning may be simple and straightforward, "There was a bug in my juice which caused me to spit out my beverage," but it is often much more complex. Causal reasoning should be used carefully, as it is difficult to indicate a causal relationship when other factors are at play. You may take protein supplements every day and state that your increased muscle mass is caused by the supplement. Since protein is a building block of muscles, this may seem like a fair conclusion. However, we must be sure to consider the other factors at play. Is the supplement alone the cause of increased muscle mass? The role of exercise cannot be ignored. Protein supplements may be a correlation and not a cause of your increased muscle mass.

For further reading on causal reasoning: https://www.researchgate.net/publication/229706112_Causal_Reasoning_Psychology_of

# Inductive Reasoning

Inductive reasoning uses a specific-to-general reasoning structure. Inductive reasoning begins with the use of specific examples (singular data) which are then studied to find patterns which suggest conclusions.

For example:

> Sleep is important for cardiac health. (Data)
>
> Exercise is important for cardiac health (Data)
>
> Good nutrition is important for cardiac health (Data)
>
> Conclusion: We have the power to impact our own cardiac health.

This conclusion is suggested, because there may be factors we have not considered, or are as yet unknown; we may have failed to acknowledge those born with heart defects, or those suffering from underlying conditions which affect the heart, etc.

The advantage of inductive reasoning is that it is easy to use, (find specific examples and look for patterns) but the disadvantage is that it cannot provide an airtight conclusion. Opponents can argue the conclusion because it is not possible to assert that every possible factor has been considered in reaching that conclusion.

# Deductive Reasoning

Deductive reasoning uses a general to specific structure. It uses something called a syllogism. There are various kinds of syllogisms, but a simple syllogism uses two premises which point to a conclusion. The first (major) premise is broad, the second (minor) premise is more specific; when both premises are valid the conclusion falls into place.

For example:

> All humans are mortal. (Major premise)
>
> Bob is a human (Minor premise)
>
> Therefore Bob is mortal. (Conclusion)

Both the major and minor premise have to be provable in order for the conclusion to be sound. Deductive reasoning can be more difficult to use, but points to a solid conclusion.

# Abductive Reasoning

Abductive reasoning is used when there is incomplete data or explanations. As mentioned in the article below, the diagnosis of an unconscious patient is an example of abductive reasoning; the doctor is making an educated guess based on his knowledge, training, examination of patient, information from outside sources, etc.

For further reading on inductive, deductive and abductive reasoning, see the tip sheet here: http://www.butte.edu/departments/cas/tipsheets/thinking/reasoning.html

# Not All Data are Processed Equally

Data can be divided into hard data and soft data. The brain processes data based on the nature of the data itself and the amount of cognitive energy it requires to process. Hard data are processed by System 2 while soft data are processed by System 1.

© VLPA/Shutterstock.com

# Hard Data

Facts

Numerical Data (Stats, Equations, Ratios, etc.)

Visual Media (Slides, Charts, Diagrams, Graphs, Videos)

## Soft Data

Narratives (Personal Stories, Business Stories)

Anecdotes

Analogies (+ All Literary Devices)

Examples (Data With a Human Face)

Descriptions

Questions: (Actual, Rhetorical, Socratic)

Humor

Music

Simple Images

© troyka/Shutterstock.com

## Why Does It Matter?

While it is difficult to measure quantitatively, it has been suggested that it takes somewhere between 2 and 7 times more brain glucose to process hard data than it does to process soft data. The brain requires additional glucose for challenging mental tasks, such as the processing of hard data (Bellisle 2004). System 2 processing tasks reduce blood glucose levels at higher rates than other mental tasks which use System 1 processing (Gailliot 2008).

This means that the audience will be exhausted more quickly when the speaker uses hard data versus soft data. Due to the limitations of cognitive load, we risk losing the audience's attention when we use too much consecutive hard data. As a speaker, you have the ability to help the audience pay attention. Unfortunately, many presentations look something like this:

Chart

Spreadsheet

Fact

Fact

Fact

Diagram

Fact

Etc.

Too much consecutive hard data are not only mentally exhausting for the listener, but also prevents them from having the mental space (available load capacity) and cognitive energy to form mental schemas from the newly acquired information. If a listener has no time to make these mental associations *during the delivery of the message* (germane load) the new information will not be retained.

There is a simple, yet not widely discussed solution to this problem and the responsibility lies fully with the speaker. The solution is that speakers be smart and intentional about information management.

# Information Management

A number of studies have found that the average attention span for listening to lectures or presentations increases within the first five minutes and then begins to decrease after ten minutes, decreasing continuously for the length of the presentation (Johnstone and Percival 1976; Burns 1985; Frederick 1986).

However, when we consider data from studies in both educational psychology and cognitive neuroscience, a clear pattern emerges. Findings indicate that attention itself is not fixed; in order to focus and maintain attention effectively, we must manage the *type* of data we use throughout the presentation, from beginning to end. The *type* of data (hard versus soft) dramatically impacts the outcome of attention, comprehension and retention (e.g., Meyers and Jones 1993; Middendorf and Kalish 1996; Olmsted 1999; Smallwood 2007; Szpunar et al. 2013).

It has been suggested that the average listener can process approximately seven minutes worth of continuous hard data before reaching mental exhaustion and needing replenishment of brain glucose. This data is qualitative and difficult to measure; regardless, the implications are clear. We must be information architects.

A conscientious speaker will avoid overloading listeners by taking two steps:

1. Limiting the use of hard data.

2. Spacing the hard data throughout the presentation.

These two steps may be accomplished by using a data ratio of 4:1 soft: hard. This ratio is based on the aforementioned implications on data processing and brain glycogen as well as on the necessary considerations of cognitive load limitations. Cognitive Load Theory suggests that we have a finite capacity to process information at any given moment in time (Chandler and Sweller 1991; Paas, Van Gog, and Sweller 2010). Since System 2 processing requires greater concentration and therefore greater mental energy, we must wisely manage the use of hard data.

While this ratio may be varied slightly according to the context, 4:1 is a "safe" ratio of hard to soft data.

# 4:1

# Soft: Hard

For every piece of hard data you use in an oral presentation, you should use four pieces of soft data. This may sound impossible, especially if you are in an industry which relies heavily on hard data; however, it is neither impossible, nor is it difficult.

The trick is to use an example after seven minutes worth of facts, or insert a quick humorous comment in the middle of a series of equations. The good news is that the brain only needs a thirty-second break to relax and allow the brain glucose to replenish itself, in order to be ready for another seven minutes worth of hard data.

Another way to manage hard data, is to change hard data to soft data. This is called re-framing the data.

Here is an example:

> "*Thirty-one percent of people prefer hemodialysis to peritoneal dialysis*" is an example of hard data.

By simply re-framing the 31 percent as an example, it becomes soft data: "*A group of people at Mercy hospital were asked about their experiences with dialysis. Only a minority of patients, 31 out of 100, said that they preferred hemodialysis over peritoneal dialysis.*"

By putting a human face on the number, it becomes an *example*, and therefore, soft data. Soft data are easier to process and intuitively preferred by the audience, based on the fact that they require less mental effort.

You will be surprised at how much easier it is to hold your audience's attention when you manage your data.

We know that audiences never retain 100 percent of content from an oral message. The real number is much, much lower. Estimates suggest that audiences retain anywhere from 5 to 30 percent of a message, but the average appears to be closer to the lower number. Because your audience is only going to recall a small portion of your content, you want to ensure that you are one who determines what that content is.

If you overwhelm your audience with hard data, there is significant risk that they become cognitively overloaded and fail to process your hard data effectively. We need to not only hold the audience's attention until it is time to reveal our best, most compelling data, we need to ensure that our best piece of hard data is processed with System 2, not System 1 processing.

This data must be placed in a particular place in the speech in order for it to have the desired effect; it should be placed at approximately the 75 percent mark in the message. At this mark, you will do two things: reveal your position and show your single, most compelling piece of hard data.

But wait. There is something you need to do right before the 75 percent mark; this action is a game-changer.

## Flip the Switch

© StockVectorsIllustrations/Shutterstock.com

At approximately the 75 percent mark, immediately before delivering your strongest, most compelling piece of hard data, you will actively flip your audience's switch. This means that you will do something to switch them from System 1 thinking to System 2 thinking. The timing of this flip is important as you want your audience to be engaged, cognitively alert, and thinking analytically and rationally to process your compelling piece of data.

> System 1: Soft Data
>
> Flip Data
>
> System 2: Best hard data

*Flip data* are questions or other types of data which require the audience to actively concentrate. Your flip data should be as engaging as possible in order to encourage participation. The purpose of this data is to move the audience from System 1 thinking into the more analytical mode of System 2.

For example:

> *"What were you doing last Thursday at 6 p.m.?"*
>
> "Which year in the past fifty years marked the greatest turning point in history?"
>
> "How many triangles can you find in this picture?"

The question must clearly have something to do with the topic at hand, but should not *in itself* be a crucial piece of information to the argument. The reason for this is that because this transition is a *changing of the guards* so to speak, moving from one system to another, the information in the transition may not be processed well in System 2. Once this system is engaged, the audience is fresh and ready for your best data. At this point, you will deliver the *strongest most compelling hard data on your side of the argument.*

# Framing

Framing is the packaging of data. Careful consideration in framing data appears to be an effective way to mitigate reactance and increase engagement.

Think carefully about how you frame information in your argument. The way that information is packaged affects the way that it is received. Consider the terms *pro-choice* versus *anti-life* and *pro-life versus anti-choice.* The terminology itself affects the perception of the message.

A surgery consent form which asks the patient to acknowledge and accept a 10 percent mortality rate, versus one referencing a 90 percent survival rate, is displaying the same information framed differently.

Always ask yourself: *What is the **best frame** for the data I wish to share?*

Sometimes, re-framing your data can make a significant difference in outcome.

Studies show that audiences will interpret messages according to the frame in which they are presented (Tversky and Kahneman 1982). These studies showed that it is sometimes advisable to frame information in a gain-frame (focusing on the positive) and sometimes in a loss-frame (focusing on risk or potential loss). Similarly, Levin, Schneider, and Gaeth (1998) showed a strong reliability factor for attribute framing, confirming that positive framing evokes positive emotions, while negative framing evokes negative emotions. Neuroimaging studies show that activation of the medial prefrontal cortex during message exposure is a reliable predictor of future behavior and gain-framed messaging showed greater activation of this region than loss-framed messaging (Vezich et al. 2016).

# Affective Strategies or Using Soft Data

Emotional appeals can be very effective in changing minds. While emotions may lead to heuristic thinking, as noted earlier, they may also serve to heighten engagement and mitigate preconceived attitudes from activating avoidance strategies (Dillard and Shen 2005).

One approach to harnessing the power of emotional responses is the use of narrative. Neuroeconomic studies show that stories encourage the production of oxytocin, which motivates empathy and cooperation (Zak 2005). Stories appear to be without persuasive intention and therefore minimize reactance and counterarguments (Moyer-Guse 2008). Listeners do not expect to be influenced by narratives and therefore their guard is down (Dal Cin, Zanna, and Fong 2004). When listening to a story, an audience does so actively, constructing the story in his own mind (Oatley 2002). This active participation increases engagement.

Studies in neuroscience confirm the positive effect of emotion in persuasion. The use of fMRI scans show that emotion activates the amygdala, which in turn intensifies engagement and subsequent memory of an event or story (Sharot 2017). Mcqueen and Kreuter (2010) found that narrative messages were much more persuasive than non-narrative persuasive messages even though high recall and behavioral intention did not always translate to actual behavior. When targeting attitudes were singled out (as opposed to behavioral intention or behavior) narratives emerged as being the most effective choice (Reinhart et al. 2007). When audiences use cognitive energies to engage with a story, they have neither the resources nor the motivation to counterargue (Green and Brock 2000; Slater and Rouner 2002). The Narrative Paradigm posits that storytelling is a more effective means of influence than logical reasoning, when that narrative has valid reasoning built into its foundation (Fisher 1987).

Research literature supports the strength of narratives in persuasive argumentation (Moyer-Guse 2008; Dal Cin, Zanna, and Fong 2004; Mcqueen and Kreuter 2010). Examined through the lens of dual process theories, the findings are supported by the theory that System 1 processing (Tversky and Kahneman 1982) is the leader of the two systems and that affective strategies are most effective by default.

When organizing a persuasive appeal, we will not only use a visceral/affective experience to begin the presentation, but will use primarily soft data for the first three-quarters of the message to minimize mental exhaustion and to maximize motivation and engagement.

The **final step** will be to transfer the information---affective experience, first nonleading question, boundary questions, best data and seed---to the message map for delivery. (See below)

### Everyday Conversation Practice

1. Try controlling the flow of a conversation with the use of boundary questions. Stated casually, they can set parameters for a discussion. For example: "*Since we're talking about whether or not to open our membership to the community*" (first nonleading question) "*I'm wondering whether or not this will increase revenue and whether or not there is danger of losing our identity if we do so...*" (boundary questions).

2. When discussing a controversial topic, at work or perhaps in a social setting, include best data from both sides. You will notice that your credibility increases in the minds of your listeners.

3. When you need to motivate someone to pay attention or to care about something, try replacing an argument with a visceral experience for your listener. While it may require some creative thinking, the benefits are worthwhile.

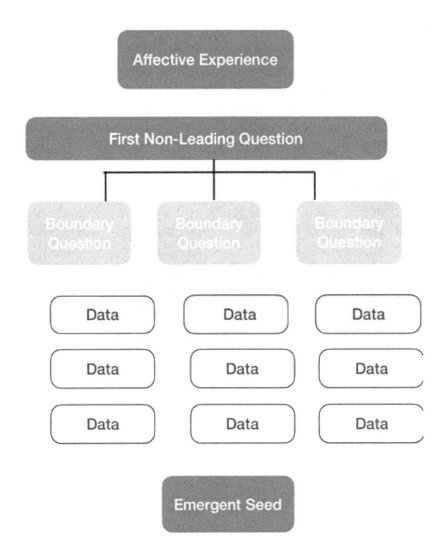

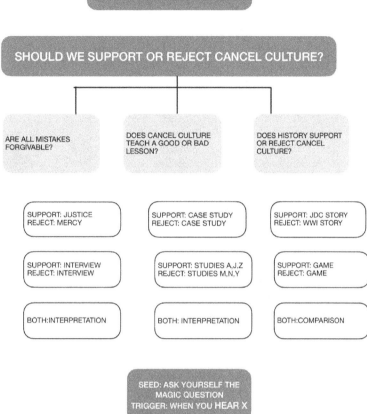

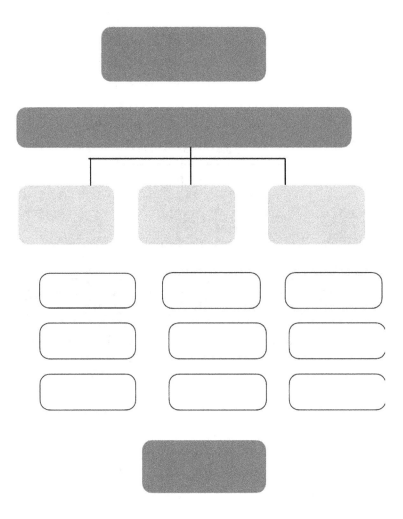

# CAFE PERSUASION: THE MICRO-PITCH

Persuasion is not reserved for stages or conference rooms. Each day of our lives we strive to exert influence on those around us. The subject matter may be trivial or profound, the stakes low or high. We persuade in cafes and banks, on trains and in bedrooms.

The principles that underlie successful persuasion allow us to understand the implications for crafting a brief appeal; our design decisions should be informed by the broad research and theories which shape the knowledge base on persuasive oral communication.

# Exerting Influence in Thirty Seconds

The ability to exert influence in thirty seconds or less is an essential skill for the twenty-first century.

Communication in the Western world is changing, with the proliferation of new media significantly affecting the way people think and behave. Changing societal constructs, values and expectations are changing the way people communicate and in particular, the way they communicate with the intent to influence.

The fast-paced tempo of the twenty-first century, the taste for immediacy and convenience has imposed new demands upon communicators: to grab attention quickly, establish purpose succinctly and clearly and deliver a message with brevity (McCormack 2014). One empirical study showed that human attention spans have decreased from 12 seconds in the year 2000 to 8.25 seconds in 2015 (Weinreich et al. 2008). While this conclusion is debatable, it is certainly true that our threshold for new stimulation has changed. The information age, while in many ways making lives easier, has created additional load and strain upon limited cognitive resources (Ophir, Nass, and Wagner 2009). As people are required to filter and process large amounts of data, they have neurologically adapted and are now conditioned to want everything faster and possess less tolerance for anything which requires patience (Yarrow 2014).

There are numerous advantages to being able to deliver concise persuasive messages. While short appeals may seem less powerful and impactful than longer arguments, there is surprising potential in brevity. Quick arguments are convenient; they are useful when time is of the essence and quick decisions must be made. Brief arguments can be a springboard for ideas.

The need for such appeals in no way lessens the need for traditional persuasive discourse, to delve deeply into concepts, to engage, explore and discuss at length. The importance of such discourse remains unchanged. Thirty-second speaking is useful in particular contexts demanded by the culture.

It is essential to consider whether or not it is reasonable to expect to exert influence in thirty seconds. While there is minimal research which addresses the primary question directly, peripheral studies may shed light on various aspects of the question.

We should recognize by now that persuasion is a process which occurs over a period of time rather than as a single event. Any information gleaned from a persuasive experience, including attitudinal shifts and behavior modifications, serves to become part of the input the next time the same topic is encountered (Nowak and Vallacher 2007). The idea of persuasion as process would appear to give value to appeals of any length, as each encounter causes the listener to further strengthen or reject an idea (Arpan, Rhodes, and Roskos-Ewoldsen 2013). As Emergence Theory applies to human learning, it also applies to the understanding of new information in a persuasive message. While thirty seconds may be insufficient to change minds completely, it is sufficient to plant a seed.

Although persuasion is understood as a process, it may be useful to consider actual consumer habits. As technology has surpassed print as the primary medium of communication, consumers have become habituated to non-linear as opposed to linear messaging and have consequently become accustomed to making quick rather than critical judgments (Postman 2007). While there is varied discussion about whether attention spans themselves are getting shorter (Anderson and Rainie 2012; Rideout 2016), Pam Briggs of Northumbria University, UK, indicates that the neural circuity in the brain is changing, based on technology usage and for most people (excluding outliers) there is an increase in mental focus using short bursts of directed concentration (Sillence et al. 2007).

Whether the changes are social or biological, new habits have led to new expectations. Busy executives demand more concise communications (McCormack 2014). Books with titles such as *What is Your One Sentence* and *Talk Less, Say More,* propose that communicators adapt their core messages for quick encounters, regardless of whether or not time is a factor (Goss 2012) because this is the age of attention management (Dieken 2010).

# TV Commercials

If the need for brief messaging is legitimate, it has been demonstrated in TV commercials.

Though dissimilar in many ways to public discourse, TV ads have a long history with the thirty-second message model. The "30-Second Effect," a study by doctors Borzekowski and Robinson (2001) was designed to measure the impact of TV commercials on participants' food preferences. Forty 2- to 6-year-olds were shown videotaped cartoons with or without commercials. They were then asked to choose one of two similar food pairs, one of which was advertised on the videotape. Children who were shown the ads were significantly more likely to choose the advertised product than the children who did not see the ads. The conclusion was that even brief exposure to an advertisement can have significant impact. Similar studies examining alcohol usage in adults confirmed these findings (Koordemanet al. 2011). Creative Chief Officer of BBDO Worldwide, David Lubars, says commercials shorter than thirty seconds produce desired effects because big ideas can be delivered in messages of any length (Lubars 2017).

© GooseFrol/Shutterstock.com

# The Elevator Pitch

While an elevator pitch may appear to be the most similar to a micro-pitch, an elevator pitch is not a persuasive appeal but an informative one (Pagliarini 2017). Informative messaging, by nature, is structured differently than its persuasive counterpart. Influencer Steve Blank states that the point of an elevator pitch is to get audiences to say "tell me more" (Blank 2014). The commonalities between the two may lie in the intention to create future interest or engagement with a topic.

# The Ingredients of a Successful Micro-Pitch

## Gaining Attention

If the aforementioned studies point to positive persuasive potential of brief messaging, one outstanding consideration is the importance of gaining full audience attention. Due to the very brief nature of the micro-appeal, time is of the essence and speaker attention is crucial from the outset.

© Alexandra Shargaeva/Shutterstock.com

There is some helpful data on how to accomplish gaining audience attention. When an individual is said to be giving his full attention, there is an intense focus on the intended object. Studies in neuroscience (Arnsten and Li, 2004) show that when humans are in this highly engaged state, they experience both desire and tension. Attention is a balance between two neurotransmitters. Dopamine is the neurotransmitter of desire/anticipation, while norepinephrine is the transmitter of tension. In order to gain full attention, it is necessary to activate both neurotransmitters by offering novelty (which will increase anticipation and an awareness of possible loss or gains, creating alertness/awareness of consequences and therefore importance) as well as creating tension or threat of loss. Dopamine neurons become more active when a reward is less likely or predictable; these neurons play a significant role in the brain signals underlying learning and decision-making. (Hollerman and Schultz 1998; Schultz, Stauffer, and Lak 2017).

## Affective Strategies

One of the differences between emotion and other cognitions is its speed. Emotions are relatively and comparatively quick. When a fast response is desirable, this is an advantage. There is of course a danger of reaching a hasty conclusion based on emotions in instances where the opposite conclusion would be reached if time had been taken for critical thought (Dillard and Peck 2000) and this is where ethical persuasion is especially important. When using emotional appeals, be sure that the audience would reach the same conclusion with additional time to process information using critical thinking. Individuals may rely solely on affective cues when a complete critical analysis of a message is not undertaken due to lack of cognitive resources, time pressures, or fatigue (Cialdini 2016).

As noted in an earlier chapter, the strength of emotional appeals, or hot cognitions, is evident.

**Hot Cognitions** are defined as data processed primarily by Kahneman's System 1 or peripheral route (emotional or intuitive) For example, stories, anecdotes and analogies are all examples of hot cognitions. **Cold Cognitions** are data processed primarily by Kahneman's System 2 or central route (critical/analytical) and include facts, statistics, graphs, etc.

Beginning a speech with a hot cognition can increase audience engagement and motivation.

## Literary Devices

It may be possible to limit an audience's resistance by changing the way they experience information. Metaphor, analogy, synecdoche and metonymy are literary devices which could prove to be particularly useful in the design of micro-pitches.

Metaphors are compact stories which can make a point in a single sentence (Van Patten 2013). Metaphor has been found to be most effective when placed in the introduction rather than later in a speech (Sopory and Dillard 2002).

It has been understood in rhetoric and communication theory that analogy has significant persuasive power (Lakoff and Johnson 1980; Whaley and Babrow 1993). Analogies may be used for a variety of purposes, but in the context of brief messaging, this includes *simplifying complex ideas* as well as *focusing understanding by avoiding long explanations* and clarifying meaning (Miller 2014).

John Mackey, CEO of Whole Foods, offsets possible objections to the high cost of natural foods by comparing Whole Foods to Starbucks. He told Fortune magazine he wanted natural foods to become as commonplace as Starbucks' lattes, which cost four dollars apiece. This comparison allowed people to see natural foods' pricing in a different light. If consumers could justify four dollars for a latte based on quality, surely they could justify high-quality food purchases.

Due to their parts-to-whole structure, both synecdoche and metonymy are effective in communicating big ideas with few words (Lakoff and Johnson 1980).

## Defining Moments

Finally, it is helpful to take a broad philosophical view of the idea of exerting influence in merely moments. There are particular moments in our lives which can be identified as defining moments, or moments which change the way we see ourselves and the world. One study identified these moments as having four factors in common: elevation, insight, pride and connection. Moments themselves are powerful; everything significant, every decision, every achievement is embedded in a moment (Heath 2017).

Based on findings of the aforementioned research in communication theory, social psychology, cognitive science and neuroscience, an optimal design for a micro-pitch has been established.

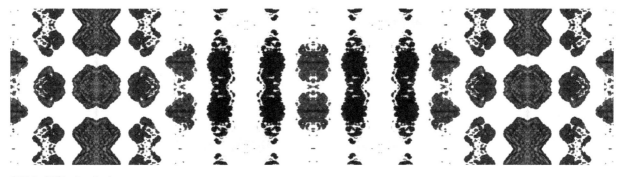

© Kate Si/Shutterstock.com

## Micro-Pitch: An Optimal Design

1. Frame the topic as a nonleading question, avoiding conclusion explicitness.

   As focused attention is crucial to the success of the micro-pitch, the nonleading question or the hot cognition which follows will incorporate the findings of previously discussed neuroscience studies on gaining maximum attention by creating novelty/anticipation to raise dopamine levels and utilizing the push--pull strategy to increase norepinephrine levels.

2.  Use a hot cognition for maximum engagement and persuasive power.

3.  Conclude with emergent data: Plant a "seed." This single piece of hard data will be chosen for its intrinsic persuasive value and potential to engage the analytical processing system to encourage continued elaboration.

While thirty seconds is brief, it is enough time to engage a listener, heighten interest, provide insight, spark discussion and raise thought-provoking questions. A micro-pitch may be thirty seconds which create a defining moment that changes the way an individual sees the world: It may be the catalyst for influence.

---

### Everyday Conversation Practice

1.  Practice the attention-gaining technique of creating novelty and using the push--pull strategy. Then practice implementing in daily conversations where you wish to maximize listener attention.

2.  Master the full micro-pitch strategy to use in daily conversation. Remember that you can exert influence in thirty seconds.

3.  Monitor your audience feedback to the micro-pitch. Are you getting the response you desired? If not, determine which aspect of the pitch you need to revise or practice.

# YOUR FACE ON THE STREET: PERSONAL BRANDING

*We all have a brand.*
*You broadcast a message to the world every day–just by showing up.*
*Do you know how people see you?*
*Do you know what you're "selling"?*
*Do you know what people would buy from you and what they would fail to buy from you?*
*Do you know why it matters?*

*This chapter is written by professional actor*
*and personal branding expert, Peter Skagen.*

## Your Public Speaking Superpower

You may have noticed that film stars are most often famous for doing the same thing in every film. You probably have a list in your mind right now. Jennifer Anniston, Tom Cruise, John Wayne from the old days. My favorite is probably Hugh Grant from the romantic comedies. It's like one long movie. This is not a criticism; it's a compliment. It means they have found their "hit" as we call it movie-acting circles, although it is also known as their brand, their sell, their sweet spot, or their superpower. As I will explain, it is critical for film actors to know and manage their hits if they hope to have lasting, successful careers. And as I will argue, it is equally critical for speakers to know their hits for all the same reasons. It is their superpower of success.

So, what is this hit? Let's imagine you are a film actor cast in a big Star Wars movie as some scoundrel. Flash forward to the premiere. Everyone is on the edge of their seat, munching popcorn, watching a teenage Yoda learn to be a Jedi master. In the middle of his *force* exercises, the door bursts open and you walk in. Within a tenth of a second the audience starts to make countless judgments and conclusions about you. Are you a good guy or a bad guy? Whose team are you on? Do they like you or not? Are they attracted to you or repulsed by you? Should they be scared or not? What do you want? What are you likely to do? This sudden crash of impressions is called your hit.

It's important to realize that this happens fast. It cracks the audience on the chin long before they are consciously aware of it. It's the "knowing without knowing" that Malcolm Gladwell points out in his book *Blink*. Before you have said a word as that space-faring rascal—and long before you have done any so-called acting—your message has already been received by the audience. Your role has already been cast. This is why actors are so fond of the saying attributed to Jack Nicholson: "Let the wardrobe do the acting." It means once you arrive on screen (as long as you have been properly cast and are executing the story) your job is largely done and the only way you can screw it up is by trying to act like the scoundrel. You already are the scoundrel. If you act like the scoundrel the audience won't see the scoundrel anymore, they will see an actor trying to be the scoundrel, which will blow the whole illusion and destroy their fun. In fact, they might despise you enough for ruining their beloved Star Wars franchise to post mean tweets all over the Internet, and run you out of the business. This is the first and most important reason actors must know and manage their hits. It is their fundamental message to the audience that makes them right for the part, and is more important than their so-called "acting."

Let me add to Malcolm Gladwell's fascinating work by explaining how and why the hit happens so fast in the movie context: The camera is a magnifying glass. If we cut back to your premiere for a moment, to your first close up, your eyeball might be 8 feet tall on that movie screen and the audience is in a state of *suspension of disbelief*, meaning they are allowing the story to pour into them unfiltered. They are completely unprotected and vulnerable, like children at bedtime and they believe that what is happening is true. Remember when you got mad at Daddy because he screwed up the story? It is the same reason fans get mad when you screw up their franchise. Your "lie" is violating their little open hearts. When your 8-foot eyeball appears on screen your hit is blasted into them point blank. Added to the fact that we humans are the greatest in the animal world for knowing what the others of our kind are thinking and you will understand just how powerful this hit can be, especially in the magnified movie context.

Just how important is the hit? Casting directors will search the world for it. Not the right actor, note, but the right person. A thousand people may audition for the role, but none will have the magic combination of looks and qualities the character must have so the open little hearts in the audience will believe. Who else on Earth but Gal Gadot could have played Wonder Woman, for example? Nobody. Who else could have played Spock after Leonard Nimoy? Only Zachary Quinto. I'm fortunate to know legendary casting director Jane Jenkins who probably cast five of your beloved movies *(Stand By Me, Ferris Bueller, Home Alone, Mrs. Doubtfire, Misery, Da Vinci Code, When Harry Met Sally, Harry Potter and the Sorcerer's Stone, Jurassic Park, Etc.)*. Well, she started her career with a little number called *The Princess Bride*, which everyone in the movie business can quote line by line. She had to look literally everywhere on Earth to find the leading lady, Buttercup. She saw all the actresses she could find, all the models, the singers, the theater stars, the girls on the street, everybody. Not one of them had the right package. Buttercup had to be regal and serene and fierce and worthy of true love and with some old-world fairytale accent and the right height to match the other actors and so on and so on…. oh and also she had to be the most beautiful girl in the world…. who could also do the acting. (And who was available and not thirty million dollars and hopefully in the union and with her US work papers). The very last person they saw was an actress with only a few credits called Robin Wright. The second she did the line "You mock my pain!" with a slight English accent, Jane said to herself "That's her. That's the Princess Bride." And so she became and so she will always be. It's impossible to imagine that movie with anyone else in the role. That is how overarchingly critical your hit is. It makes or breaks you long before the acting begins. You must be right for the part or the audience will not buy your story.

Let's do a demonstration. You are now making a movie. My uncle paid for it, and suggested you look at me for a role. Have a look at my headshot and cast me. That's my headshot right there. It doesn't matter what the movie is about. Just look at that mug staring at you and consider what message it broadcasts in your mind. Am I a good guy, a bad guy, or somewhere in the middle? Do you like me or not? Trust me or not? What am I likely to do? Do I shoot guns, give orders, fly spaceships, kiss girls, get killed, or cause the death of others? Am I high status or low status? White collar or blue collar? Am I in contemporary movies, or period movies? Movies or television? What kind of movies or television shows can you imagine me in? Or do I appear in commercials? What products do I sell? Trucks, financial products, Viagra? What do you think? What do you believe? What do you want?

Who I think I am doesn't matter; it's about who you believe I am. Take a moment to come up with a few answers.

Okay?

Here's what you said: Male, Caucasian, about 50-something, good guy/bad guy, a high-status wild card, intimidating, white collar or blue collar, capable of violence, contemporary and period, does movies and TV shows like *Breaking Bad*, and is never seen doing commercials unless he's selling hand grenades. I'm a bit Clint Eastwood-y and a bit Jack Nicholson-y. That's my basic hit.

How do I know? Two reasons. First: Whenever I do a lecture or a class, I ask the audience. For thirty years they have all given me the same answers regardless of their demographic. Second: You can look at my resume on IMDB.com where you will see all the roles I've done are variations on this list. That's the audience voting with their eyeballs.

To be an actor, speaker, or anyone in the public eye who frequently or occasionally appears on screens is to be confronted by this reality, and sometimes it stings. I may have wanted desperately to play Romeo, for example, but I was never right for Romeo even at twenty years old. I might have gotten away with it on stage, but never on screen. For one thing, I had those scars you see on my face at that time too and they just don't sell Romeo. Nor does my essential nature (the other half of my hit) which you can also read in my photo. Everything counts as we will see. To be a success is to embrace not just what you want but what the audience wants as well. You must give your gifts to those who want your gifts. You cannot force yourself on the audience. You must become congruent.

Some hits are broader than others, the broadest of all being likeability. Tom Hanks is the likeable, everyman, American prince. The audience will therefore accept him in all sorts of roles—good guys, bad guys, romantic comedy leading men, religious mystery detectives, and children's TV icons—as long as the character is likeable, American, and princely. Sandra Bullock is the female equivalent. Clint Eastwood is the destroyer god Shiva. He's the good guy who is "badder" than the bad guys for a good cause. His hit is very narrow (essentially the same character in all his films) but likewise very powerful. Johnny Depp is the quirky, outsider, leading man. Cate Blanchett is the goddess. Leo is the tragic Prince. Morgan Freeman is God.

**Your hit is comprised of two basic things: your look and your feel, also known by some in LA as your silhouette and essence, or just your inside and your outside.** According to Marty Neumeier's seminal book, *The Brand Gap*, it works exactly the same way for all product brands: **half intrinsic value and half design**.

Your look is itself comprised of two things: your basic look (White? Black? Asian? Six foot twelve? Missing an eye? Conjoined twin?) and your presentation (Wearing a purple kilt for some reason? Bad hair and makeup day? Speaking Pig Latin? Angry at the world?).

Your feel is also comprised of two things: the obvious combination of the nature and nurture that made you who you are on the inside, which is pretty much cooked by the end of high school and the less obvious contribution of your shadow or subconscious mind, which you are by definition unaware of, but which the audience can see.

Let's unravel these one at a time.

If you walk into a room naked, it will matter to the people in that room. If you walk in with a machine gun and a clown mask, it will matter even more. So, what you look like matters. There is not some magic point at which it matters while the rest of the time it doesn't. We wear uniforms to make it matter less, but it still matters. I am often accused of being threatening because I have mean eyebrows. I have scars on my face and scars are always scary to people because they imply some violence. I'm also rather tall and broad, so I am always slightly or overtly scary to people I meet. Sure, over time they may come to disregard the eyebrows and scars, but it takes time and effort to overcome the original power of your hit and you ignore it at your peril (and when under stress, people will tend to revert to their original feelings about you). Rather, if you are fully aware of your hit, you can manage it for the benefit of all.

You can modify your look one way or the other by how you present it. A smile and open, engaged body language helps everyone come across more disarming and likeable, even me. Being appropriately dressed, well-groomed and minty fresh help too. Speaking slowly and confidently while keeping engaged eye contact wins most every time. Nose rings, face tattoos, mirrored sunglasses, shaving the left half of your head and carrying a flaming machete are all distractions and barriers, which will make you harder or impossible to read and embrace. My wonderful uncle, Kenny, was a salesman who always dressed crisp and dapper. He even ironed a crease in his jeans. When I asked him about it he said: "When you dress badly, people look at your clothes. When you dress well, people look at you." That's a good summary.

While your look can be modified and will change over time as you age, your *feel* cannot. Until you attain complete Buddhahood (and perhaps even afterward) you are who you are, resulting from your nature and nurture into maturity. Clint Eastwood is the same intimidating good guy/bad guy with a code at 90 as he was when he began at 25. He will never suddenly become Jim Carrey. I still recognize my daughter from when she was one year old. Your look, of course, is quite obvious; your feel is less obvious but equally powerful. We instantly love some people we meet; others just rub us the wrong way. Individual responses to the inner you may vary, but the audience's collective response will be strikingly consistent over time.

Finally, we must venture into the minefield of your shadow, or subconscious mind. This subject is best described by the psychologists of course, but I can again give you the perspective of the magnifying-glass camera. There is a reason why you can give your friends advice, but can't seem to figure out your own life: You can see into their shadow, while they by definition cannot. You know them better than they know themselves. And should your friend be magnified by the camera and projected onto a big screen, that shadow would be blasted into you in Technicolor with surround sound. You won't see a bullet-list of detail, of course, but you will see and feel enough to know its depth and probable intent, and you will also see how your friend is unaware of it. The most compelling film stars tend to have the biggest shadows, because it makes them unpredictable and fascinating and we love to watch them contend with those shadows. Think: Robert De Niro, Christian Bale, Angelina Jolie, James Dean and Marilyn Monroe. These actors are not "putting on" a shadow; they have been well cast.

In real life, people with the most shadow are the most unsettling, whereas people with the least shadow are the most obvious and embraceable. They are predictable and thus non-threatening. Humans are comfortable around all things obvious and predictable, like a nice tree and uncomfortable around all things opposite of a nice tree, like a hyena or a serial killer.

As any good shrink will tell you, you are controlled by your shadow and thus are completely unpredictable even to yourself and therefore dangerous. Deep-shadow people tend to be complicated outsiders and even criminals until they integrate those shadows into their conscious minds, at which point they tend to become leaders and billionaires owing to the character-building they have endured.

No matter the depth and breadth of your shadow, your audience will see it. It is therefore the most important element of your hit to investigate, because it ultimately has the most impact. You may be handsome, charming, well-dressed and generally likeable, but people will still respond most to that cesspool of darkness (or bright lift of love) they feel in the background.

How do you become aware of your shadow and the rest of your hit? Again, we can consult the psychologists for the clinical perspective and I can give you instruction on how we do it in the movie world.

The number one best way is to go directly to the audience and ask them. This is known as a screen test. We simply put you on screen in a particular way and read the results. Feedback from a live audience is best because you can feel them as well as they feel you. You know when they are speaking the truth. You can ask questions. As an audience put into "storyland" by the movie screen, they are naturally inclined to respond to you strongly, to cast you and want to help you. I do screen tests as the foundation of all my workshops and can tell you that fifteen minutes of feedback from an audience can be life-changing for people.

A quicker exercise is to choose the actor/celebrity/billionaire you most admire (not the one you want to date) and make a list of their personal qualities. Because we admire people we identify with, that list will describe you, too, giving you a glimpse of your feel and shadow. It's pop psychology, but it can be instructive.

If you want to get your pals involved, you can also do what I call the box-of-wine test. Invite six or eight friends over for a drink. About twenty minutes later casually slip this question into the conversation: "Hey guys, if they were making a movie of my life, who would play me?" You might want to casually take notes into your phone as they say something like: "Oh my gosh, Angelina! She's so dark and mysterious and dangerous and screwed up." It's important here not to fight back, but only to encourage feedback and take notes. You can laugh or cry later. They are telling you your basic hit. (You are well advised then to watch all Angelina's films and look for more clues and common threads.) Then try this question: "What does she have to do to win in the end?" Take more notes as they say something like: "Oh, she has to stand up for herself and learn to trust people." They are revealing your immediate challenge and parts of your shadow. And if you can ask one more, it would be: "Who's the bad guy?" The bad guy, or antagonist, in every movie is the magnetic opposite of the hero. Like Darth Vader, he has all the skills, knowledge and *force* powers Luke lacks but has to acquire in order to become who he is and win in the end. Luke needs to become Darth Vader in other words (without staying on the *dark side*) in order to become a *Jedi*, a hero and the man he was meant to be. Thus, we get to see our hero integrate his shadow on screen before our eyes, which is the main thrill and enlightenment of the movies. Take more notes and then let the conversation drift off to something else. Only later will you examine those notes and watch those movies for insight.

If you happen to be an actor, you can examine your resume, read your old reviews and talk to your directors. If you are an experienced speaker, you can ask leading questions on your feedback forms, organize post-show focus groups, or plant spies in the audience to gather intelligence on your behalf. But the best way of all is the good, old screen test.

It takes courage and an open mind to find and embrace your hit. You may find it is exactly what you thought it would be, or that is exactly what you didn't think it would be. It's no fun learning that everyone hates your glasses and that you've been dressing like the judge in a porn movie for that last ten years. It's challenging to accept that parts of you are in shadow, that you are unaware of yourself and controlled by a foreign power. It can be embarrassing and ostracizing and uncomfortable. But just like your credit card debt, it is better to know than to be willfully ignorant. You can begin to manage it and start the process of integration by becoming progressively more aware. The most integrated, or congruent, people are the most powerful, influential and successful people.

As a speaker, you will almost certainly be on screen as you speak and likely posted to YouTube later, so all the same principles apply. In addition, you can design your presentation based on your hit, knowing in advance what the audience wants to buy from you. You can use your hit as the locus of your power. If your hit is long on charm, for example, you can sprinkle it throughout like a good dramaturge would (being careful not to overuse it) and really turn it on for your big finish. You can use your sensitive introversion to elicit a deep emotional response to your message. If you are naturally forceful and intimidating, you can balance it out with goofy props or self-deprecating jokes. You can completely disarm an audience by admitting right away that you come across like a creepy video store clerk. You can invite them to check out your dark side and laugh at your humanity. Being vulnerable and authentic—and most of all congruent with them—is the surest way known to win over an audience and influence their decisions. If you are worried that this is all just so much manipulation, do as the actors do. Think of it all as generous storytelling, as good teaching, as caring for the audience. Consider your personal brand to be an important aspect of yourself—important enough to investigate. Know and manage your brand, because when your brand sells, so too will your message.

Peter Skagen is a working film and television actor, international coach, and author of the award-winning book *Screen Acting Trade Secrets.*

### Everyday Conversation Practice

1.  Try one of the exercises in this chapter to discover your brand.

2.  Manage your brand to fit the image you wish to project. Small changes can make a big difference. If you want to become a politician but people see you as having a "shady" vibe, you may need to shave your facial hair, lose the glasses, smile more often, increase your vulnerability and use more personal narratives, all with the intent of making yourself appear more trustworthy to your audience. Remember, you may be the most honest guy in the world, but if people perceive you differently, you need to do something about it. Manage your brand.

# KIOSK:
# SALES TOOLS

We are always selling.

We sell products, ideas, services and we sell ourselves.

© isaxar/Shutterstock.com

While contemporary wisdom dictates that we should avoid being overly "sales-y" in our pitches, the literature in both psychology and business marketing provides important insights for effective message design.

The *Prospect* Awareness Scale was developed by Eugene Schwarz and explained in his book *Breakthrough Advertising* (1966). While this scale was first intended for marketing purposes, it applies equally to all prospects or audiences. We are always selling; sometimes we sell products or services, but mostly, we sell ideas.

While the scale is important to both informative and persuasive communication, it is crucial in the art of sales. It is essential to identify our specific audience's level of awareness so that we may successfully target their attention and interest.

# What is the One Belief?

*What is the one belief that your audience needs to hold in order to desire your product/ service or idea?*

Identifying this one belief is crucial at the outset of developing your message.

# Prospect Awareness Scale

## Fully Aware

Fully aware that your idea/product is the best option; repeat "customers."

## Idea/Product Aware

Aware that your idea/product is the best choice but needs more data.

## Solution Aware

Aware of the potential solutions; unaware of which solution is best.

## Problem Aware

Senses that there is a problem, but doesn't know where to find a solution.

## Unaware

No knowledge that a problem or need exists

*At what level of awareness is your audience, at this moment in time?*

There is a big disconnect that occurs when we address an audience at the wrong level of awareness. For example, imagine "Sales-Guy Roy" speaking to a small group of young adults in their 20s. He is selling an anti-inflammatory ointment for the gums called *Gingivax.*

**Roy**: *Gingivax is the best ointment on the market to reduce inflammation in the gums. It is the only product of its kind on the market which does not contain benzenes. It is also less expensive than the alternatives...*

Roy thinks that he is addressing some very important concerns and making his product stand out from the rest. This is good, but he is missing something much more important. Safer and cheaper—sounds like a done deal! Maybe not. What these young adults really need to know is this: *Why do I need ointment for my gums in the first place?*

Here is the problem. As soon as Sales-Guy Roy starts talking, one of the listeners turns to his friend and says, "*What is this guy talking about? Inflammation in your gums??*" His friend likely responds the same way. Why? Because young adults don't even know that inflammation in gums is a problem. It doesn't relate to them, or so they think. Even if Roy explains at the end of the presentation that this issue is relevant to them at this point in their lives, it is too late. People have already tuned out because they don't want to waste cognitive resources listening to something that doesn't apply to them.

Now what if, instead, at the beginning of his pitch, Roy says *"I know you guys probably work hard to stay healthy, eating well and exercising regularly. Did you know that inflammation in your organs is one of the leading causes of disease and that this inflammation begins to become problematic when you are in your 20s? Do you know where a lot of this inflammation starts? In your mouth."*

Now, the audience is listening. This time, Roy has addressed the audience at the bottom of the awareness scale. He is presenting them with the problem. He is making them *problem aware.*

In the first example, Roy was trying to jump right to *product awareness* and it didn't work.

If Sales-Guy Roy had asked himself, *what is the one belief that my audience needs to hold in order to desire my product?,* he would have realized that the answer is the need to believe *that they need this product at this time in their lives.*

Always begin at the level above your audience's awareness level. If your audience is unaware, begin by telling them the problem. If the audience is problem aware, begin by discussing possible solutions to the problem. If they are solution aware (meaning they are aware of all possible options already), explain why your product or idea is the best choice. If they already know the best option, elaborate with details to make them fully aware.

© Dmitriip/Shutterstock.com

# Sales Techniques

Here are ten techniques which are easy and effective to use when selling products, services or ideas:

## Distinction

Imagine walking into a big box store like Target or Walmart with the intention of shopping for a household product to clean your kitchen sink. When you enter the cleaning aisle, you are overwhelmed with a hundred products which are all designed to do the same thing: clean kitchen sinks. The question which confronts you is *which product should you choose?* It is in this moment of decision that a brand's message design decisions will affect the choice that you make. You will choose the product that stands apart or is distinct to you, personally.

For example, if you desire that your kitchen sink be sparkling white, you may be inclined to purchase a bottle that features one of those "sparkle" symbols. The sparkle aligns with your vision of what you want the product to accomplish.

The next person who enters the aisle looking for a product to clean their sink might look only at price, scanning the tags and choosing the cheapest one. This shopper might not even glance at the bottles themselves. Each of you will purchase a product based on distinction, or the product which stands out to you, personally, from the others. Note that what makes a product distinct is different for each of you.

Design your product, service, or idea with distinction in mind. Ask yourself, *how will mine stand apart from the others? Is my product cheaper, more cutting-edge, lighter, sleeker, etc.?* When it comes to selling ideas, you must do the same. Ask yourself how your version of the message is different or unique to other versions of the same message which your audience may have heard numerous times before. This aligns with the latitude of noncommitment. This is especially important with frequently discussed topics so that your audience doesn't immediately tune out because they think they have heard it all before.

## Scarcity

While scarcity can be an example of heuristic thinking (scarcity heuristic), it can also be legitimate motivation to encourage response. In its heuristic form, we value something more when it is unavailable or less easily available to us (Lynn 1992). In principle this is a mental shortcut as opposed to a form of rational thinking because valuation is dependent upon availability (an external factor) rather than on the merit of the object/idea itself. The error lies in the assumption that something less available must be more valuable than something which is more easily available.

However, this technique may be used ethically as long as it adheres to the standards of persuasion (in the listener's best interest) and not manipulation (in the salesperson's best interest). While the seller must benefit from a sale, ethically speaking, he should not benefit at the cost of harm to the consumer.

Scarcity works effectively when the seller offers a product for a limited time, or offers only a limited number of products.

Scarcity can be used by a speaker in a similar way to suggest a limited time to accomplish a task:

*"If you want to be a millionaire, you need to start investing when you are in your 20s."*

*"We need to save the Black Rhino before it goes extinct. Time is of the essence."*

## Social Proof

Human beings are influenced by the opinions of others. We can see this in our own tendencies to check Trip Advisor or Google Reviews, etc., to inform our opinions prior to making a purchase. A Nielsen survey in 2015 confirmed that the most credible advertising comes from those we know; we are most likely to purchase based on recommendations from friends or family. This is called positive social proof.

© Fears/Shutterstock.com

While positive social proof is effective, negative social proof is not. In other words, don't tell somebody not to do something if everyone else is doing it. Cialdini et al. conducted a study (Cialdini, Goldstein, and Martin, 2008) in the Arizona Petrified Forest. Park authorities had noticed that many visitors were taking a piece of wood home as a souvenir, so the researchers posted two signs asking visitors to refrain from stealing the wood. The first sign simply asked people not to steal wood, while the second version of the sign effectively said that *many people were stealing wood*, so please don't do it. The actual amount of wood stolen was gauged using marked pieces of wood. The results of the study were astonishing. The second sign resulted in almost triple the amount of thefts compared to the first sign. Why? Because when you tell people that many other people are engaging in a behavior, this makes the behavior more popular!

# Reciprocity

In social psychology, reciprocity means returning a kindness or good deed with the same. There is strong tendency to feel that we owe another person something when they do something good for us. If your friend Bill helped you move into your new apartment last year, you will likely feel obligated to help him move when you find out that he is moving residences.

When it comes to selling a service or product, we can use reciprocity by offering a gift, a deal, a free session, etc. Reciprocity in the realm of ideas may be more subtle, such as offering to concede on an idea in a negotiation or even by using a friendly delivery style. Your listeners will be inclined to smile back at you and respond with more positive nonverbal signals if you yourself have made an effort to be friendly.

# Pain Point

This is a deep psychological need which motivates our desire to make a purchase. It is connected to an emotional need, beyond the physical need that may be obvious. For example, we buy toothpaste to clean our teeth, which is a physical need, yet there is an underlying pain point which motivates this desire. We may want clean teeth in order to feel attractive, to avoid rejection, etc. An individual who wants to improve his business presentations so that his voice is heard in the workplace may be identifying judgment as a pain point. If his voice is not being heard, he will feel that he is not appreciated or valued. That emotional pain is at the root of his desire for change.

By identifying your audience's pain point, you can target your arguments to solving his problem.

# Cost-Benefit Analysis

Cost-benefit is the principle of economics which states that in order for a transaction to take place successfully, the consumer must believe that the intended benefit of the product or service will outweigh the cost incurred. This is an intuitive principle and we use it frequently to make decisions. If you are buying a used car, which has high mileage and makes a clunking sound when you drive it, but is being sold for a very low price, you need to believe that the benefits of the car outweigh both the financial cost and the risk of buying a lemon.

Cost-benefit applies to ideas as well. When we choose to adopt a new perspective or change our behavior, there is always a cost involved. The cost in this case is not usually financial, rather it may be a cost of time, or even a cost of giving up our old familiar ideas.

As a persuasive speaker, you need to make sure that your audience views benefits as greater than costs. Don't pretend the costs do not exist. Acknowledge them and show how they are worthwhile due to the anticipated benefits.

## Anchoring

Anchoring is actually a cognitive bias, whereby we interpret future information based on a previous reference point, where that reference point may or may not be relevant. For example, when participants in two studies were asked if they thought Gandhi was over or under a particular age when he died, and then asked his actual age at death, the students responses clustered closely around the age suggested. When the question of his age at death was asked to a different group of participants without the prior reference to a specific age, the answers were across a much broader range. The mention of the specific age anchored their responses (Mussweiler and Strack, 1997, 2001).

Anchoring, although it is a bias, may be used to suggest a reference point when that reference point may be helpful. For example, a realtor who suggests an asking price is essentially establishing an anchor. The expectation is that the offers made will be close to the asking price. Suggested donations are another use of anchoring.

When referring to ideas in a message, a speaker may use anchoring to provide suggested boundaries or expectations. For example, a speaker who is asking his colleagues to familiarize themselves with the new office software, may suggest that his colleagues attempt to use the software five times in the subsequent week. Some individuals may try it four times and others six or seven times, but five suggests a boundary reference point.

© Anton Kustsinski/Shutterstock.com

# Foot in the Door

Foot in the door technique was coined by Freedman and Fraser in 1966 and was based on a study designed to prove their theory that a substantial request has a much greater chance of being granted when it follows the acceptance of a smaller request. The study consisted of a control group and an experimental group, both which were asked to display a large unattractive sign on their front lawns saying either *Drive Safe* or *Keep California Beautiful.* In the control group who were asked to display the large sign as the initial request, less than 20 percent of participants agreed to the request. For the experimental group, however, the initial request was to place a small sign in their window. Once they agreed, the homeowners were visited two weeks later and only then asked to place the large sign on their lawn. In this case over 55 percent of participants agreed to the large sign request. This theory aligns with the idea that humans like to be consistent; once we have agreed to a first request, we are likely to agree to a second similar request.

Sales people often use this technique by handing out free samples. Once you have accepted a beauty product sample, for example, they may ask if they can quickly apply a product to your face or hands. Saying yes once increases your likelihood of saying yes a second time.

# Door in the Face

While in principle, this technique is the opposite of the previous one, both techniques work effectively and choosing when to use which will depend on the context.

Door in the face technique is used when a speaker starts by asking for the larger request first and when that has been denied, she follows it with a smaller, usually more reasonable request. The psychology of saying yes to the second request is often a matter of guilt in denying the first request. Imagine that you ask your friend to donate 100 dollars for a good cause. He says no, because he is a poor student. Then you ask him to donate just 5 dollars; this time he will be inclined to respond in the affirmative. The 5 dollars seems like a small request when compared to the earlier larger request.

# Danger of Incentives

While there is significant data on the finding that the use of incentives may be a poor idea in many circumstances, the use of incentives remain popular. Let's examine when incentives are useful and when they are dangerous.

Imagine that your boss asks you to work over the weekend to complete a project. He tells you that if you do, he will give you 300 dollars. You think that sounds fair, so you complete the work. It appears as though the incentive has worked and it has, but...what about next month when he asks you to work on the weekend, but there is no mention of compensation? How are you going to react when you find out that there is no money involved? While incentives work in the short term, they actually have a negative effect in the long term. In a study conducted with elementary school students, incentives were counter-productive when offered as reward for reading (Stanfield 2008). Various studies have shown that rewards produce temporary compliance, but decrease intrinsic motivation in the long term (Deci and Ryan 1985; Freedman 1966).

One interesting finding was that a bonus offered after the fact, did not have the same negative effect as incentives offered as a condition in advance. In the example used above, if your boss asked you to do the work without any promise of compensation, but then *after* if it was completed, offered you a *surprise* bonus to say thank you, your perception would be different. Because the work was not *contingent* upon the money, you would not lose the intrinsic motivation to take on extra work in the future.

In other words, if you don't care about anything but short-term motivation, use incentives, but if you care about long-term motivation, use nonconditional bonuses in lieu of rewards.

**Sales techniques are tools for your speaking arsenal; with practice, you will be able to discern how, when and where to use these tools to increase your sales, regardless of whether you are selling products, services or ideas.**

---

### Everyday Conversation Practice

1. Sell an idea by using one of the techniques from this chapter.

2. Combine two techniques to sell an idea.

3. Begin to target your listeners using the Prospect Awareness Scale. This technique is surprisingly helpful even in everyday conversation.

---

# STREET TOOLS

# Priming

Robert Cialdini calls priming "pre-suasion" or the art of influencing minds prior to the delivery of a message (Cialdini 2016). Priming works at a subconscious level, often without our knowledge. For example, if you drove by a fried chicken restaurant this morning, you may not consciously recall seeing the restaurant and think that your craving for fried chicken at dinner time is a random craving.

Priming happens on many levels. Imagine that you need a new doctor and search RateMyMD.com to find a recommendation. You notice that Dr. Taylor has very high ratings and so you proceed to book an appointment with him. Because you have been primed to like the doctor (due to his high ratings) your actual experience with him will be colored by that impression. You may excuse his tardiness, *He's popular, that's why he's so busy, so I don't mind waiting. You* may even excuse his rude behavior and find excuses for it because you have been primed to see the doctor in a positive light.

# Magic Questions

There are two questions which we ask ourselves, prior to making a behavioral intention or adopting a new behavior. The questions are: *Am I capable? Is it worth it?*

Imagine that your cousin asks you to try parkour with him on the weekend. Parkour involves using the obstacles in your environment to move from place to place and frequently involves jumping from rooftop to rooftop. Before you agree to join your cousin, you will subconsciously ask yourself whether or not you are capable. If you love high-risk sports and you are in great shape already, you might answer in the affirmative without giving much second thought. If you don't consider yourself to be a good fit for the sport you will reject the offer. The second question, *Is it worth it,* involves an evaluation of risk, challenge, etc. If you are considering applying to law school, you will likewise ask yourself these two questions. If you think that you are both capable (sufficient intelligence and self-discipline) and you think law school is worth it (the cost, the long hours, the lack of social life, etc.) then you will take action. If you say no to either question, the decision ends there.

Since we know that people ask themselves these questions, as an influencer, we can pre-emptively answer the questions for our audience, before they ask themselves, by confirming to them that they are both capable and that the suggested idea is indeed worthwhile. Clearly, we should always remember the ethics of providing honest and realistic information to the target audience.

© Zeljkica/Shutterstock.com

# Single versus Joint Evaluations

When delivering a message which requires a decision on the part of your listener, consider carefully what kind of decision you want them to make---an emotional decision or a logical decision. Choice architecture allows us to nudge consumers in a particular direction based on the way the information is presented. While a relatively new field of study, evaluations are known to be an important piece in decision-making and awareness of how evaluations lead to particular kinds of decisions can determine how you present options (LU Xi 2018).

In a study conducted by Kahneman and Ritov (1994) researchers asked for donations to two separate charities: save the dolphins and cancer research. The results differed depending on how the options were presented. When potential donors were asked in isolation to donate to save the dolphins (a single evaluation), they raised more money than when donors were asked, again in isolation, to donate to cancer research. In other words, when asked to donate separately to each cause, people were willing to donate more money to saving animals than to saving humans. However, when the two options were presented together, the results were different. This time, people gave more money to cancer research. Why? When donors were forced to compare the two options, they used critical thinking skills, rather than relying on emotional decision-making. They realized that while dolphins are important, that cancer research for humans might be a more rational choice.

Studies have shown that people are more likely to make an emotional decision when presented with a single evaluation (one option, or a series of isolated options) and they are more likely to make a logical decision when presented with a joint evaluation, or two or more options presented in tandem (Kahneman and Ritov 1994). Because the presentation of two or more options is comparative in nature, it leads to the activation of System 2 thinking rather than the System 1 or default thinking used with a single evaluation.

# Positive Deviance

In the book *Influencer: The New Science of Leading Change* (Grenny et al. 2013), there is a story about researcher Dr. Donald Hopkins who worked diligently in order to eradicate guinea-worm disease from the planet. Guinea-worm disease is caused by drinking water infected with worm larvae. Upon ingestion, the larvae hatch, grow and eventually burrow out of the body causing great pain and suffering. No cure or medications exist. When Dr. Hopkins started his research, three million people in twenty countries were being infected every single year. Hopkins visited a number of African villages which were hotspots for the disease. He also identified a single village in the same geographical region which had *not* seen an outbreak, in other words, an outlier. By following individuals in both the infected and uninfected areas to observe their daily habits and rituals, he was able to identify behaviors practiced in the clean village as compared with the behaviors in the infected areas. What he determined was a simple difference, yet one with a profound impact. In the infected villages, the women would source water from a nearby river by scooping water from the river directly into buckets and carrying them home to their families. In the uninfected village, however, the women would go to the same river in pairs and while one would scoop the water into the bucket, the other woman would hold out her skirt and the first woman would pour the water through her skirt into the bucket. Then they would trade positions. Hopkins was witnessing the most basic filtration system—a system which was keeping the inhabitants of the village healthy. What he identified is called *positive deviance*—the vital behaviors which cause a positive result where others in the same circumstances have achieved a negative result.

In the business world, positive deviance might be determining why one small oil company has survived in a climate where other small oil companies were forced to shut their doors. Finding the vital behavior that is responsible for a different outcome is positive deviance.

© kapooklook01/Shutterstock.com

# Social Capital

Studies show that if you wish to achieve a goal, perhaps losing weight or completing a dissertation, that you are more likely to succeed at the goal if you use social capital (Helliwell et al. 2017). In other words, tell everyone about your goal and encourage them to encourage you (Grenny et al. 2013). Social capital is a way to use others' influence to make ourselves accountable for our own behavior. If you are attempting to stick to a daily exercise routine, you might ask your friends to send you quick texts of encouragement, perhaps saying things like *"Day 16! So proud of you,"* or *"don't forget to go for your run today."* Social capital is a powerful way to ensure follow through when setting goals.

# Fear Only with a Solution

While fear can be a powerful human motivator, it has been shown to have positive impact only when used in the context of offering a solution or alternative. The Scared Straight program was designed to turn juveniles away from a life of crime, by showing them the high probability of getting caught and being prosecuted. The juveniles were taken to a prison and shown their potential fate through the lives of prisoners. Unfortunately, in its inception, the program left out a crucial part of the message: "If you change your ways, you won't have to go to prison in the first place!" Perhaps the organizers hoped that the participants would draw this conclusion themselves, but that is not what happened. Following participation in the program, participants' criminal behavior actually increased and they seemed more worried about not getting caught than not committing crime in the first place. When the program implemented revisions to clearly communicate that there was another option and how to pursue that option (normal employment, a life free of crime) only then did fear work as a positive motivator (Grenny et al. 2013).

## Consider Changing Things

While it is common to focus on changing attitudes, beliefs, or behavior, it is easy to overlook the simple and effective method of exerting change by changing *things*. One familiar study showed that people eat less when they change their dinnerware.

According to the Mayo Foundation for Medical Education and Research (Hensrud 2018), people eat smaller portions when they simply choose a smaller plate. This was confirmed by additional studies including one such study by Hughes et al. (2017). Changing things can include the placement of offices within a building, the size of a computer monitor, the packaging of an item, etc. The possibilities are endless and the results are promising.

© Anastasiia Lapteva/Shutterstock.com

# Power of Narrative

While the use of affective strategies has been discussed at length in an earlier chapter, it is important to mention that stories have the greatest power to influence due to the neurochemical changes that take place in a listener's brain when they hear a story. First-person stories are more effective than third-person stories because of the inherent authority in telling a story about something that happened to you directly.

© balwanrai/Shutterstock.com

Specificity is the key to achieving impact with your stories. Narratives about individual people tend to be more powerful than stories about generic groups. For example, if you want your listeners to donate money to a charity which supports needy women and children in Bangladesh, don't just tell a story about "women and children." Tell a specific story about a woman and her children. Give them names and faces. When we hear a story about "children starving" we feel helpless, because it seems like an overwhelming problem. When we hear about Mary and her three kids, we feel that maybe we can make a difference after all.

St. Teresa of Calcutta (Mother Teresa), although she dedicated her life to helping the poorest of the poor, was known for her focus on helping one person at time. Focus on the individual, not the group.

# Address the Why

As Simon Sinek suggests, we should always start with *why* (Sinek 2009). People need to know *why* they should pay attention, *why* they should take action, *why* they should avoid a certain behavior. Human behavior depends on motivation and if we are not given a motivation, we will either think that one does not exist or we will invent our own explanation, which often is erroneous.

Imagine that you are on holidays with a group of friends. After a night out walking on the beach, you decide to take a late night swim in the hotel pool, However, when you reach the hotel's outdoor pool, you see a sign that says *"No Swimming after 10 p.m."* Since it is now after 11 p.m., you are technically forbidden from swimming, but you don't see a good reason for this prohibition. None of you have been drinking and you are all proficient swimmers. You collectively decide that it is just a stupid rule because there are no lifeguards on duty, so you hop in the pool.

Now, what if you knew that at 10 p.m., the pool is infused with toxic chemicals for cleaning. Would knowledge of that one simple fact change your behavior? For most people, the answer is yes. If the sign had stated *"No Swimming: Chemical Pool Cleaning from 10 p.m.–10 a.m."* the *why* of the prohibition would be clear and compliance would increase dramatically.

Here's a short video from **Simon Sinek: Start With *Why* To Inspire Action**
**https://www.youtube.com/watch?v=HjriwYrGL28**

# Focus On Behaviors Not Outcomes

Organizations are often accustomed to using an abstract "outcome-based" focus, rather than a behavioral focus when designing goals. The problem with outcomes is that they tend to be vague, broad and lack clear directives for change.

Take this outcome for example: *This university is committed to diversity.* This may sound good on paper but what does it actually mean? How does being committed to diversity look? How do we accomplish this? Outcomes tend to be *passive* while behaviors are *active*. A behavior should be stated from an action perspective: *This university will do X, Y, and Z to ensure the representation of diverse populations.* While it may be inferred that an action will be *developed* from an intended outcome, these outcomes may be too easily buried in the proliferation of wordy, abstract documentation that is filed away and forgotten ultimately resulting in a lack of direct action.

# Connect Behaviors to Values

When we wish to ask someone to undertake a behavior, especially if that behavior is difficult or requires significant change or sacrifice, it is a good idea to tie that behavior to the individual's values. Tying the behavior to *your* values is not the same as connecting them to your audience's values. For example, you may want your Uncle Dan to stop drinking excessively because he shows up at your parties and embarrasses you; but if you ask him to change his behavior based on your reason (the value of self-image/self-protection) you are approaching the ask from a rather selfish (although perhaps justified) perspective. It would be better to identify your Uncle Dan's values. What is important to him? Perhaps he is raising a small daughter as a single parent. If you know that his daughter means the world to him, you could tell him that you know how important she is to him, that you are certain he wants to be around to see her grow up and that if he drinks too much, that may not be possible.

© Vanzyst/Shutterstock.com

# If Construction

When discussing hot-button issues, issues which are highly controversial and which may be met with increased resistance, the *If construct* allows a speaker to introduce potentially controversial information.

For example, instead of stating "*Bob Jones was visited by an angel*" a controversial idea which will certainly be met with some skepticism, a speaker may state that "*Bob Jones claims to have been visited by an angel*" and point out that the fact of visitation is either true or untrue, based on the problem of noncontradiction which by virtue of logic dictates the statement to be either true or false.

The speaker will then ask the audience to **consider the possibility** of the information being true. *I ask you to play along with me for a few minutes and consider this—what if it's true that Bob was visited by an angel? What does that mean for us here...?*

Generally people are more willing to consider an idea when it is not presented as being forced upon them, but when they are asked to engage, almost in a playful manner, to consider controversial data.

© Perunika/Shutterstock.com

# Specified Listening

Sometimes our persuasion attempts fall on deaf ears because we do too much talking and not enough *listening*. The most effective way to reach our audience is to be aware of their existing attitudes on the particular issue we are discussing. It has long been suggested that most people are attached to their viewpoint because of *one primary reason.* This idea may be better understood by looking at the philosophical classifications of motivating reason and explanatory reason (Alvarez 2009, 2017). Ask your listener why they believe what they do, before you start to speak. Listen carefully. They will usually offer their primary reason *first*. This is the area on which you should focus your message. The fact that they will follow the first reason with other reasons is simply a matter of justifying their position; this is due to the human desire to remain consistent and committed to a position. Sometimes you may be surprised at someone's primary reason for adhering to a position and may be pleased to find your task of helping to change their mind easier than expected.

# Spot The Inarguable

Spotting the inarguable allows the speaker to begin a conversation on a point of similarity. This is an intelligent choice as common sense would suggest that listeners are more inclined to engage in a discussion when the tone is amiable rather than confrontational.. Find a point on which you and your listener agree. For example, let's say you are discussing the topic of teachers potentially having guns in classrooms. Instead of getting into a debate which focuses on your differences and encourages defensive arguments, find a point on which you and your listener agree. For example, "*I'm sure we both agree that saving lives is paramount.*" When your listener agrees, try to find another point of similarity as you lead your way through the conversation.

A key point to remember when using this approach is that you don't want to introduce dissent until absolutely necessary. If dissent arises, return to a major point of agreement and try to discuss from there. For example, "*Ok since we both agree that saving lives is important, what do you think is the best way to ensure that lives are saved...?*"

# Peak—End Rule

Peak--End Rule suggests that we best recall information which occurs either at the end or at the most intense point of an experience (Tversky and Kahneman 1999). This phenomenon is so powerful that it can affect our perception of memory. In one study, colonoscopy patients recalled experiences as *less painful* when pain levels were moderate to high throughout the procedure but dropped for the last minute of the procedure than other patients with had low pain throughout and a pain spike at the end who ranked the pain level as being *higher* (Redelmeier and Kahneman 1996). Perceptions are influenced by placement of information.

Think about a holiday you took five years ago. What do you remember today about that holiday? According to these findings, you likely remember the end of the trip and the highest and lowest moments. "*Oh that was the time we saw the whales....* or "*That was the time that Joe broke his leg.*" When planning a holiday, if you plan to travel for five days and have a total entertainment budget of 1,000 dollars, it would seem to make sense to allocate 200 dollars for each day. With this data in mind, however, you may wish to reconsider how you allocate the money. It might be better to splurge on one memorable activity and spend a little more at the end of the trip. Apparently those days in between are forgettable anyway!

# Analogy

Analogy is a comparison of two ideas based on their similarities. Perhaps you don't understand the role of lysosomes and proteasomes in the human body but if you are told that they are like the neighborhood garbage collectors it is easier for you to understand microbiology.

Analogies are particularly useful in persuasive communication (Whaley and Babrow 1993; Sopory and Dillard 2002). In a study which examined the effect of analogy on attitude change, subjects were exposed to either figurative, literal or no-analogy messages. They found that both the literal and figurative messages resulted in greater attitude changes than the no-analogy messages (McCroskey and Combs 1969).

Analogies are particularly helpful when discussing controversial issues where confirmation bias might be problematic. When people are resistant to changing their position, they may stop listening to an opposition argument. We want to prevent or eliminate negative emotional reactions regarding topic-specific content. Analogies allow us to make a point *using a different topic* and then revert back to the original topic and reference the same point.

For example, if Bob struggles with obesity, he may not want to listen to another conversation about his weight. As soon as you approach the subject of diet, he may stop listening.

If, however, you approach the topic by asking Bob a simple question: *Bob, as my friend, If I were walking backward toward a steep cliff, but wasn't aware that I was doing it, would you tell me?*

Bob will say yes, if he is your friend. Then you confirm that you would do the same for him, because you care about him. Then bring the analogy back to the topic you *really* want to discuss. *Bob, I see obesity as coming close to stepping off a cliff. It's dangerous and I care about you.*

When the desired point has been made, it smooths the path forward.

# Deadlock Strategy

Deadlock Strategy is a technique that is used when you are not progressing in a conversation on a controversial topic. It involves three steps: (1) Identify a hidden assumption in the other party's argument; (2) Use that assumption in an analogy to make a point; (3) Return to the original topic and refresh the point. The benefit of this strategy is that it allows you to make a point outside of the actual topic being discussed. The reason that this is important is because it diffuses the emotional defense mechanism which arises when your opponent disagrees with you. Changing to a new topic increases engagement (use of novelty) and reduces your opponent's need to defend his position.

© Rayyy/Shutterstock.com

Let's say that the university you attend has canceled a guest speaker when they discovered that she held controversial opinions on the topic of her presentation. You have a discussion with the student president.

Start by identifying a hidden assumption in this argument. Remember that this is not something that the speaker has stated explicitly, rather a *hidden* viewpoint that underlies their argument. *"So what you are saying is that we should not allow controversial ideas to be freely expressed at a university."*

After she agrees with your statement, use that assumption in a new topic. *"So what about textbooks which provide controversial viewpoints? Should those also be disallowed?"* (*Now return to your topic with this point.*) *"If we shouldn't disallow this, then why are we restricting freedom of speech?"*

(In this example, the analogy was fairly close to the topic itself, but the analogy can also be further away from the topic, as long as it is a reasonable comparison.)

# Linking States

Linking States is a neurolinguistic programming or NLP technique. It is rooted in the fact that human beings do not change emotional states dramatically when presented with new data. An attempt at moving the audience too quickly to a new emotional state often results in failure. Instead, guide the audience to move gradually from their current state to the desired state. This gradual move through emotional states is called linking states. For example, if your audience is currently apathetic about the topic of fundraising for ALS research, it is almost impossible to move them from apathy to excitement in one step. Ask yourself what is between the state of apathy and the state of excitement and then work to move the audience from apathy to the next most positive state, which may be curiosity. Once they are curious. you may try to move them from curiosity to interest. Once they are interested, then you may be successful at moving them from interest to excitement.

# Against My Better Judgment

This technique uses the power of vulnerability, while simultaneously leveraging the opposition position as a point of similarity. For example, if you are against the idea of prisoners having the right to vote, but your opponent is for it, you will gain a lot of credibility in her eyes if you admit to once holding her viewpoint and admitting that you only changed your mind, against your own better judgment. In other words, you'd rather have stayed on her "side" but the evidence forced you to change your views. This technique is useful if you did indeed change your mind, but should not be used to pretend otherwise if it is not the case.

**There are many techniques from which to choose. Part of being a successful persuasive speaker depends on your ability to discern when and where to use each technique. Familiarize yourself with the variety of tools and incorporate them into daily conversations so that they become a part of your repertoire.**

---

**Everyday Conversation Practice**

1. Try implementing one technique at a time into your ordinary conversations.

2. Combine one technique with a nonleading question, framed within your listener's latitude of noncommitment.

3. Discern when and where to use each technique by noticing appropriate moments to implement them.

# STREET-FIGHT:
# NEGOTIATE

Negotiating is tricky business. While traditional wisdom on negotiating relied on rallying ideas back and forth until you eventually met your opponent somewhere in the middle, new research and strategies suggest a different approach.

Don't meet in the middle. Chris Voss is a former FBI lead international kidnapping negotiator and CEO of the Black Swan Group, where he works to solve business negotiation problems using hostage negotiation strategies.

In his book, *Never Split the Difference*, Voss suggests the following strategies for negotiation.

# Mirroring

While you may be familiar with mirroring as a nonverbal technique (synchronizing your voice and body language with those of your counterpart), mirroring in the art of negotiation primarily focuses on the *verbal* mirroring of ideas.

As a general guideline, let the other party speak first. Listen carefully to your opponent's ideas and then paraphrase his words back to him using three key words to summarize his main idea. Oftentimes in the English language, the main point comes at the end of a sentence.

Once you have repeated the three key words, be silent. Your silence will encourage your opponent to do one of two things: either agree with you or clarify their statement. Your silence encourages elaboration.

© Dmitriip/Shutterstock.com

Use "**I'm sorry**" to begin a sentence when mirroring something with which you disagree or where you need clarification. "I'm sorry" is an implicature—which is a word or phrase used to soften a statement. While we generally want to avoid implicatures in our speech, as they can weaken our statements, negotiations are high-stakes, high-emotion communication. Using an implicature right before a challenging statement will soften what may otherwise appear as a confrontational approach.

> **Manager**: *We need the project completed by this Friday.*
>
> **You**: *I'm sorry, completed by this Friday?* (Silence)
>
> **Manager**: *Yes, we were hoping to have it done by Friday.*
>
> **You**: *I'm sorry, you're saying by Friday.* (Silence)

At this point in the conversation, the mirroring technique followed by silence will provoke the manager to reflect upon his request and re-calibrate his thoughts.

The re-calibration will ideally result in a pivot to change his request.

> Manager: *Well, how about next Friday; would that work?*

© Iva1/Shutterstock.com

Note the importance of silence within this interaction. If we use "I'm sorry" and the mirroring technique without following it with silence, we fail to allow our opponent to re-calibrate and the conversation will not move forward in a productive manner.

# That's Right

Chris Voss explains that when we agree with something someone is saying, we don't say "you're right" we say "that's right." Voss discovered from working in the field as an FBI negotiator that when people say "you're right" they are at a place where they want you to stop talking and go away. Rather than indicating what the literal meaning would suggest, there is a subconscious negative undertone to these words.

The words "that's right," however, trigger a chemical change in the brain which makes us feel that we have been heard and understood. If you can get someone to say "that's right" they are actually giving you a signal that they believe that you appreciate their viewpoint.

This technique should be used with repetition. The more often an opponent says the words "that's right" the more they believe that the two of you are on a path to clear and empathetic communication on the topic.

# Labeling

Human beings desire to be understood. Labeling helps uncover facts that drive the person's behavior while suggesting empathy and understanding of their position. Labeling uses the power of empathy to connect with an opponent and move a negotiation forward. Labeling begins with active listening; we must listen not only for literal statements, but attempt to read between the lines to determine how our opponent is feeling and try to identify the direct cause of those emotional responses. Labeling is the verbal observation of the other's feelings.

> *"It sounds like you are hesitant to move forward."*
>
> *"It sounds like this is really bothering you..."*
>
> *"It looks like you don't think this is a good idea."*

After labeling a feeling, go silent. This silence will encourage the speaker to keep talking. Every time the opponent speaks, you gather important information.

If you mislabel your opponent's feelings, either unintentionally or intentionally, the technique still works effectively because the natural response is for the opponent to correct the error and re-calibrate.

For example:

> **You**: *"It looks like X is really bothering you."*
>
> **Opponent**: *"It's not that X is bothering me; what's bothering me is Y."*

Listening to the responses of the other side is crucial as these responses will allow you to break down the components of their position and allow you to make deliberate choices about your next move.

Here is a short video demonstration on mirroring and labeling:

**https://www.masterclass.com/classes/chris-voss-teaches-the-art-of-negotiation/chapters/exercise-mirroring-and-labeling#**

© Grenar/Shutterstock.com

# Calibrated Questions

Calibrated questions are open-ended questions beginning with the words *what* or *how*.

A question starting with the word *why* can seem confrontational and should be avoided. It's often possible to re-frame a *why* question using *what*. For example, instead of asking *"why did you choose to do this"* we may re-frame as *"what made you choose to do this"* and we will ultimately end up with the same response.

Follow a calibrated question with silence. Then listen.

Certain calibrated questions are useful in any negotiation situation because they make the other party feel respected. Here are a couple of suggested questions that Voss uses as default questions in most negotiations:

*What is really important to you?*

*How would you like me to proceed?*

# Tone of Voice

According to Voss, people are six times more likely to make a deal with someone they like. A positive frame encourages likability. He suggests using a positive, friendly tone of voice 95 percent of the time---a voice with a smile.

The other 5 percent will be reserved for cases where you need to state something as an absolute. He terms this voice the late night DJ voice—calm, deep and authoritative.

# No

Don't be afraid of hearing your opponent say the word "no." According to Voss, "no" is not the end of the conversation, but the beginning. Saying the word "no" gives the speaker a sense of control and security. When they feel safe and comfortable they are more likely to offer information and elaborate. In a negotiation, knowledge is power. The more information we acquire the more conscious deliberate choices we can make.

Allowing "no" to be a part of the conversation is important because it slows down the conversation and gives you time to think and react in a logical rather than emotional manner.

# Yes

Just because someone says "yes" doesn't guarantee that they *mean* "yes."

# Three Kinds of "Yes"

## Counterfeit

The person really wants to say no, but feels pressured into saying yes.

For example:

> You are a customer in a high-pressure sales conversation. You may feel the pressure to tell the salesperson that you will be back tomorrow to buy the product (yes) when you really have no intention of doing so. Yes, in this case, is a form of escape.

## Confirmation

An innocent reflexive "yes "to a straightforward question.

For example:

> **George:** "You like coffee, right?"
>
> **Sally:** "Yes."

This kind of yes doesn't mean much as it is a reflexive response that doesn't require thought or commitment.

© Boguslaw Mazur/Shutterstock.com

## Commitment

This is the "yes" that we want to hear in a negotiation. It signals commitment to our idea. The problem is that it *sounds* the same as the other versions of "yes" listed above. In order to be able to differentiate which "yes" we are receiving, it is necessary to practice listening for the different kinds of affirmative responses in various situations, so when we hear the three types, we recognize them for what they truly represent.

# Leverage

Leverage is the ability to withhold gain and inflict loss. It may be considered "situational power." The CEO of the company at which you are employed, may have absolute power over you and your role at the company, but if you are parked directly behind him in the parking lot, it is you who hold the situational power, or leverage.

Ask yourself the following questions:

*What does the other party want to gain?*

*What do they fear losing?*

Voss describes leverage as water sloshing between two parties. Whoever feels like they have most to lose at any given moment has less leverage.

# Types of Leverage

## Positive

When the other party wants something, you have leverage. You can offer them some version of what they desire.

## Negative

When the other party fears losing something, you have leverage. Loss aversion is a powerful psychological motivator. Human beings make choices which minimize loss. In fact, in most circumstances, we are more likely to make choices which minimize loss over those which maximize gain (Kahneman 2011).

Due to the fact that negative leverage is essentially using threats, this might be a good place to remind ourselves of *ethics*. People don't like to be threatened, so use this technique wisely, after considerable thought and weight given to the pros and cons.

## Normative

Normative leverage begins with developing an understanding of the other party's values and standards. People like to remain consistent within their own set of values and if there is a potential discrepancy between their values and their behavior, normative leverage may be an effective way to move the discussion.

For example, if Joe places a high value on honesty, yet is avoiding telling the truth about his tax evasion, reminding Joe of his own standards will cause him to experience cognitive dissonance, or an awareness of imbalance.

**Negotiator**

Joe, I know that being honest is really important to you so I am inviting you to tell me what happened with your taxes.

The discrepancy will be evident to Joe and the human need to remain consistent with one's own values and behavior may motivate him to tell the truth.

While each of these techniques may be used alone, they have greater negotiation power when used together.

While negotiating is an art unto itself and may be studied in greater depth, the techniques discussed here will enable you to incorporate negotiation strategies in both formal communication as well as in informal everyday conversation.

As always, practice is the key to mastering any technique. If we use techniques in conversational speaking, we will be comfortable and ready to use them in higher-stake negotiation situations.

---

## Everyday Conversation Practice

1. Try the mirroring technique in an ordinary conversation.
2. Try the labeling technique when engaged in a high-emotion conversation.
3. Begin using calibrated questions to help clarify your conversation partner's ideas and wishes.
4. Once you have mastered individual techniques, try combining them.

# CITATIONS

## Why

Ajzen, Icek. "The Theory of Planned Behavior." *Organizational Behavior and Human Decision Processes* 50, no. 2 (1991): 179-211. doi:10.1016/0749-5978(91)90020-t.

Ajzen, Icek, and Martin Fishbein. "A Bayesian Analysis of Attribution Processes." *Psychological Bulletin* 82, no. 2 (1975): 261–77. doi:10.1037/h0076477.

Rhodes, Nancy, and David R. Roskos-Ewoldsen. "Outcomes of Persuasion: Behavioral, Cognitive, and Social." In *The SAGE Handbook of Persuasion,* 2nd ed., edited by J. P. Dillard and L. Shen, 53–69. Thousand Oaks, CA: SAGE, 2013.

Roskos-Ewoldsen, David R. "Attitude Accessibility and Persuasion: Review and a Transactive Model." *Annals of the International Communication Association* 20, no. 1 (1997): 185–225. doi:10.1080/23808985.1997.11678942.

## Street Talk: The Power of Questions

Beckman, A. "Hiding the Elephant: How the Psychological Techniques of Magicians Can Be Used to Manipulate Witnesses at Trial." Scholarly Commons @ UNLV Law, 2014. Accessed March 24, 2018. http://scholars.law.unlv.edu/nlj/vol15/iss2/11/.

Brehm, Sharon S., and Jack W. Brehm. "Persuasion and Attitude Change." *Psychological Reactance* (1981): 121–50. doi:10.1016/b978-0-12-129840-1.50010-7.

Brehm, Sharon S., and Jack W. Brehm. *Psychological Reactance: A Theory of Freedom and Control.* New York: Academic Press, 1981; 2013.

Buller, David B., Michael Burgoon, John R. Hall, Norman Levine, Ann M. Taylor, Barbara Beach, Mary Klein Buller, and Charlene Melcher. "Long-Term Effects of Language Intensity in Preventive Messages on Planned Family Solar Protection." *Health Communication* 12, no. 3 (2000): 261–75. doi:10.1207/S15327027HC1203_03.

Chaiken, Shelly. "Heuristic versus Systematic Information Processing and the Use of Source versus Message Cues in Persuasion." *Journal of Personality and Social Psychology* 39, no. 5 (1980): 752–66. doi:10.1037//0022-3514.39.5.752.

Cruz, M. G. "Explicit and Implicit Conclusions in Persuasive Messages." In *Persuasion: Advances through Meta-analysis*, edited by Mike Allen and Raymond W. Preiss, 217–30. Cresskill, NJ: Hampton, 1998.

Deci, Edward L., and Richard M. Ryan. "The Support of Autonomy and the Control of Behavior." *Journal of Personality and Social Psychology* 53, no. 6 (1987): 1024–037. doi:10.1037//0022-3514.53.6.1024.

Dillard, James Price, and Lijiang Shen. "On the Nature of Reactance and Its Role in Persuasive Health Communication." *Communication Monographs* 72, no. 2 (2005): 144–68. doi:10.1080/03637750500111815.

Heath, Chip, and Dan Heath. Simon and Schuster, 2017. https://books.google.ca/books?id=4O-vDgAAQBAJ&pg=PA98&lpg=PA98&dq=chip+and+dan+heath+shit+latrine+defecation&source=bl&ots=UbcUzM2IAC&sig=ACfU3U05BFmfO6J2yUSk6_28WhsvErSLcg&hl=en&sa=X&ved=2ahUKEwib3PuE3JbqAhU0HzQIHeB9Do4Q6AEwAXoECAoQAQ#v=onepage&q=chip%20and%20dan%20heath%20shit%20latrine%20defecation&f=false

Hovland, Carl I., and Wallace Mandell. "An Experimental Comparison of Conclusion-drawing by the Communicator and by the Audience." *The Journal of Abnormal and Social Psychology* 47, no. 3 (1952): 581–88. doi:10.1037/h0059833.

Jowett, B. (2010). *Dialogues of Plato.* New York, NY, NY: Cambridge University Press.

Petty, Richard E., Zakary L. Tormala, and Derek D. Rucker. "Resisting Persuasion by Counterarguing: An Attitude Strength Perspective." *Perspectivism in Social Psychology: The Yin and Yang of Scientific Progress* (2004): 37–51. doi:10.1037/10750-004.

Lydon, John, Mark P. Zanna, and Michael Ross. "Bolstering Attitudes by Autobiographical Recall." *Personality and Social Psychology Bulletin* 14, no. 1 (1988): 78–86. doi:10.1177/0146167288141008.

Niederdeppe, Jeff, Hye Kyung Kim, Helen Lundell, Faheem Fazili, and Bonnie Frazier. "Beyond Counterarguing: Simple Elaboration, Complex Integration, and a Counterelaboration in Response to Variations in Narrative Focus and Sidedness." *Journal of Communication* 62, no. 5 (2012): 758–77. doi:10.1111/j.1460-2466.2012.01671.x.

O'keefe, Daniel J. "Standpoint Explicitness and Persuasive Effect: A Meta-Analytic Review of the Effects of Varying Conclusion Articulation in Persuasive Messages." *Argumentation and Advocacy* 34, no. 1 (1997): 1–12. doi:10.1080/00028533.1997.11978023.

Paul, Richard, and Linda Elder. "Critical Thinking: The Art of Socratic Questioning." *Journal of Developmental Education* (2007). Accessed March 24, 2018. https://www.questia.com/library/journal/1P3-1447133181/critical-thinking-the-art-of-socratic-questioning.

Petty, Richard E., and John T. Cacioppo. "The Elaboration Likelihood Model of Persuasion." *Communication and Persuasion* (1986): 1–24. doi:10.1007/978-1-4612-4964-1_1.

Petty, Richard E., and John T. Cacioppo. "Effects of Forwarning of Persuasive Intent and Involvement on Cognitive Responses and Persuasion." *Personality and Social Psychology Bulletin* 5, no. 2 (1979): 173–76. doi:10.1177/014616727900500209.

Reich, J. W., and J. L. Robertson. "Reactance and Norm Appeal in Anti-Littering Messages." Journal of Applied Social Psychology 9, no. 1 (1979): 91–101. doi:10.1111/j.1559-1816.1979.tb00796.x.

Rosenberg, Benjamin D., and Jason T. Siegel. "A 50-Year Review of Psychological Reactance Theory: Do Not Read This Article." *Motivation Science* (2017). doi:10.1037/mot0000091.

# East to West: The Mysterious Business of Changing Minds

Miller, Gerald R. "Afterword." *Message-Attitude-Behavior Relationship* (1980; 2002): 319-27. doi:10.1016/b978-0-12-199760-1.50016-9.

Roskos-Ewoldsen, David R. "Attitude Accessibility and Persuasion: Review and a Transactive Model." *Annals of the International Communication Association* 20, no. 1 (1997): 185–225. doi:10.1080/23808985.1997.11678942.

Sherif, Carolyn W., Muzafer Sherif, and Roger E. Nebergall. *Attitude and Attitude Change*. Westport, CT: Greenwood Press, 1965; 1981.


# Streetlight: Illuminating Thinking and Decision-Making

Ajzen, Icek. "The Theory of Planned Behavior." *Organizational Behavior and Human Decision Processes* 50, no. 2 (1991): 179-211. doi:10.1016/0749-5978(91)90020-t.

Ajzen, Icek, and Martin Fishbein. "A Bayesian Analysis of Attribution Processes." *Psychological Bulletin* 82, no. 2 (1975): 261–77. doi:10.1037/h0076477.

Beebe, S. A., and S. J. Beebe. *Public Speaking Handbook.* New York: Pearson, 2018.

Carpenter, Christopher J. "Using Spinozan Processing Theory to Predict the Perceived Likelihood of Persuasive Message Claims: When Message Recall Matters." *Southern Communication Journal* 83, no. 1 (2017): 1–12. doi:10.1080/1041794x.2017.1373146.

Chaiken, Shelly, and Alice H. Eagly. "Communication Modality as a Determinant of Message Persuasiveness and Message Comprehensibility." *Journal of Personality and Social Psychology* 34, no. 4 (1976): 605–14. doi:10.1037//0022-3514.34.4.605.

Chaiken, Shelly. "Heuristic versus Systematic Information Processing and the Use of Source versus Message Cues in Persuasion." *Journal of Personality and Social Psychology* 39, no. 5 (1980): 752-66. doi:10.1037//0022-3514.39.5.752.

Dutton, K. *Split-Second Persuasion: The Ancient Art and New Science of Changing Minds*. Boston, MA: Houghton Mifflin Harcourt, 2011.

Eagly, Alice H., and Shelly Chaiken. *The Psychology of Attitudes.* Belmont, CA: Wadsworth Cengage Learning, 2010.

Evans, Jonathan St. B. T., and Keith E. Stanovich. "Dual-Process Theories of Higher Cognition." *Perspectives on Psychological Science* 8, no. 3 (2013): 223–41. doi:10.1177/1745691612460685.

Festinger, Leon. *A Theory of Cognitive Dissonance*. Stanford, CA: Stanford University Press, 1957; 2009.

Gass, Robert H., and John S. Seiter. "Chapter 2: What Constitutes Persuasion?" In *Persuasion, Social Influence, and Compliance Gaining*, 34–35. Boston, MA: Allyn and Bacon, 2003, 2011.

Heath, Chip, and Dan Heath. Switch: How to Change Things When Change Is Hard. London: Random House Business, 2011.

James, W. "What is an emotion?" *Mind* 19 (1884): 188–204.

Kahneman, Daniel. *Thinking, Fast and Slow*. London: Allen Lane, 2011.

Petty, Haughvedt and Smith. (2014). Elaboration as a Determinant of Attitude Strength. In R. E. Petty & J. A. Krosnick (Authors), Attitude strength antecedents and consequences. New York: Psychology Press, Taylor & Francis Group.

Petty, Richard E., and John T. Cacioppo. "Effects of Forwarning of Persuasive Intent and Involvement on Cognitive Responses and Persuasion." *Personality and Social Psychology Bulletin* 5, no. 2 (1979): 173–76. doi:10.1177/014616727900500209.

Petty, Richard E., and John T. Cacioppo. "The Elaboration Likelihood Model of Persuasion." *Communication and Persuasion* (1986): 1–24. doi:10.1007/978-1-4612-4964-1_1.

Petty, Richard E. "Creating Strong Attitudes: Two Routes to Persuasion." *PsycEXTRA Dataset* (2017). doi:10.1037/e495742006-014.

Tversky, Amos, and Daniel Kahneman. "Judgment under Uncertainty: Heuristics and Biases." (1981) *Science* 185, no. 4157, 1124-131. doi:10.1017/cbo9780511809477.002

# Roadblocks: Biases, Heuristics and Fallacies

Buller, Burgoon, Hall, Levine, Taylor, Beach, Klein Buller & Melcher (2000) Long-Term Effects of Language Intensity in Preventive Messages on Planned Family Solar Protection, Health Communication, 12:3, 261-275, doi: 10.1207/S15327027HC1203_03.

Chaiken, Shelly. "Heuristic versus Systematic Information Processing and the Use of Source versus Message Cues in Persuasion." *Journal of Personality and Social Psychology* 39, no. 5 (1980): 752–66. doi:10.1037//0022-3514.39.5.752.

Chambliss, Marilyn J., and Ruth Garner. "Do Adults Change Their Minds after Reading Persuasive Text?" *Written Communication* 13, no. 3 (1996): 291–313. doi:10.1177/0741088396013003001.

Chandler, Paul, and John Sweller. "Cognitive Load Theory and the Format of Instruction." *Cognition and Instruction* 8, no. 4 (1991): 293–332. doi:10.1207/s1532690xci0804_2.

Dillard, James Price, and Lijiang Shen. "On the Nature of Reactance and Its Role in Persuasive Health Communication." *Communication Monographs* 72, no. 2 (2005): 144–68. doi:10.1080/03637750500111815.

Deci, Edward L., and Richard M. Ryan. "The Support of Autonomy and the Control of Behavior." *Journal of Personality and Social Psychology* 53, no. 6 (1987): 1024–037. doi:10.1037//0022-3514.53.6.1024.

Fransen, Marieke L., Edith G. Smit, and Peeter W. J. Verlegh. "Strategies and Motives for Resistance to Persuasion: An Integrative Framework." *Frontiers in Psychology* 6 (2015). doi:10.3389/fpsyg.2015.01201.

Gladwell, M. *Talking To Strangers: What We Should Know About the People We Don't Know.* Penguin Books, 2020.

Kahneman, Daniel. *Thinking, Fast and Slow.* London: Allen Lane, 2011.

Lydon, John, Mark P. Zanna, and Michael Ross. "Bolstering Attitudes by Autobiographical Recall." *Personality and Social Psychology Bulletin* 14, no. 1 (1988): 78–86. doi:10.1177/0146167288141008.

Niederdeppe, Jeff, Hye Kyung Kim, Helen Lundell, Faheem Fazili, and Bonnie Frazier. "Beyond Counterarguing: Simple Elaboration, Complex Integration, And A Counterelaboration in Response to Variations in Narrative Focus and Sidedness." *Journal of Communication* 62, no. 5 (2012): 758–77. doi:10.1111/j.1460-2466.2012.01671.x.

Paas, F., T. van Gog, and J. Sweller. "Cognitive Load Theory: New Conceptualizations, Specifications, and Integrated Research Perspectives." *Educ Psychol Rev* 22 (2010): 115–121. https://doi.org/10.1007/s10648-010-9133-8.

Petty, Richard E., and John T. Cacioppo. "Effects of Forwarning of Persuasive Intent and Involvement on Cognitive Responses and Persuasion." *Personality and Social Psychology Bulletin* 5, no. 2 (1979): 173–76. doi:10.1177/014616727900500209.

Petty, Richard E., Zakary L. Tormala, and Derek D. Rucker. "Resisting Persuasion by Counterarguing: An Attitude Strength Perspective." *Perspectivism in Social Psychology: The Yin and Yang of Scientific Progress* (2004): 37–51. doi:10.1037/10750-004.

Tversky, Amos, and Daniel Kahneman. "Judgment under Uncertainty: Heuristics and Biases." *Science* 185, no. 4157 (1974): 1124–131. doi:10.1017/cbo9780511809477.002.

Wason, P. C., and Philip Nicholas Johnson-Laird. *Psychology of Reasoning: Structure and Content.* London: BT Batsford, 1972.

# Construction: A Fire Pentagon

Bellisle, F. "Effects of Diet on Behaviour and Cognition in Children." *British Journal of Nutrition* 92, Suppl. 2 ( 2004): 227–32.

Burns. Ralph A. "Information Impact and Factors Affecting Recall." Annual National Conference on Teaching Excellence and Conference of Administrators (7th, Austin, TX, May 22–25, 1985).

Chandler, Paul, and John Sweller. "Cognitive Load Theory and the Format of Instruction." *Cognition and Instruction* 8, no. 4 (1991): 293–332. doi:10.1207/s1532690xci0804_2.

Dal Cin, S., M. P. Zanna and G. T. Fong. 2004. "Narrative Persuasion & Overcoming Resistance." In *Resistance and Persuasion*, edited by E. S. Knowles and J. A. Linn, 175–91. New Jersey: Lawrence Erlbaum Associates Publishers, 2004.

Dillard, James Price, and Lijiang Shen. "On the Nature of Reactance and Its Role in Persuasive Health Communication." *Communication Monographs* 72, no. 2 (2005): 144–68. doi:10.1080/03637750500111815.

Fisher, Walter R. "The Narrative Paradigm: An Elaboration." *Communication Monographs* 52, no. 4 (1987): 347–67. doi:10.1080/03637758509376117.

Frederick, P. "The Lively Lecture: Eight Variations." *College Teaching* 34, no. 2 (1986): 43–50.

Gailliot, M.T. "Unlocking the Energy Dynamics of Executive Functioning: Linking Executive Functioning to Brain Glycogen." *Perspectives on Social Science* 3(2008): 245–63.

Green, Melanie C., and Timothy C. Brock. "The Role of Transportation in the Persuasiveness of Public Narratives." *Journal of Personality and Social Psychology* 79, no. 5 (2000): 701–21. doi:10.1037//0022-3514.79.5.701.

Johnstone, A. H., and F. Percival. "Attention Breaks in Lectures." *Education in Chemistry* 13 (1976): 49–50.

Levin, Irwin P., Sandra L. Schneider, and Gary J. Gaeth. "All Frames Are Not Created Equal: A Typology and Critical Analysis of Framing Effects." *Organizational Behavior and Human Decision Processes* 76, no. 2 (1998): 149–88. doi:10.1006/obhd.1998.2804.

Mcqueen, Amy, and Matthew W. Kreuter. "Women's Cognitive and Affective Reactions to Breast Cancer Survivor Stories: A Structural Equation Analysis." *Patient Education and Counseling* 81 (2010). doi:10.1016/j.pec.2010.08.015.

Meyers, C., and T. B. Jones. *Promoting Active Learning: Strategies for the College Classroom.* San Francisco: Jossey-Bass Publishers, 1993.

Middendorf, J., and Alan Kalish. "The Change-Up In Lectures Natl. Teach. Learn." Forum, 1996, tchsotl.sitehost.iu.edu

Mighton, John. "Chapter 2: The Emergent Mind." In *The End of Ignorance: Multiplying Our Human Potential*, 25–35. Toronto: Vintage Canada, 2008.

Moyer-Guse, Emily. "Toward a Theory of Entertainment Persuasion: Explaining the Persuasive Effects of Entertainment-Education Messages." *Communication Theory* 18, no. 3 (2008): 407–25. doi:10.1111/j.1468-2885.2008.00328.x.

Oatley, Keith. "Chapter 3: Emotions and the Story Worlds of Fiction." In *Narrative Impact: Social and Cognitive Foundations*, edited by Melanie C. Green, Timothy C. Brock, and Jeffrey J. Strange, 39–41. New York: Psychology Press, Taylor and Francis Group, 2002.

Olmsted, J. A. "The Mid-Lecture Break: When Less Is More." *Journal of Chemical Education* 76 (1999): 525–27. doi: 10.1021/ed076p525.

Paas, F., T. van Gog, and J. Sweller. "Cognitive Load Theory: New Conceptualizations, Specifications, and Integrated Research Perspectives." *Educational Psychology Review* 22 (2010): 115–21. https://doi.org/10.1007/s10648-010-9133-8.

Reinhart, Amber Marie, Heather M. Marshall, Thomas Hugh Feeley, and Frank Tutzauer. "The Persuasive Effects of Message Framing in Organ Donation: The Mediating Role of Psychological Reactance." *Communication Monographs* 74, no. 2 (2007): 229–55. doi:10.1080/03637750701397098.

Sharot, Tali. "Chapter 2: Emotion: How We Were Persuaded to Reach for the Moon." In *The Influential Mind: What the Brain Reveals about Our Power to Change Others*, 41–44. New York: Henry Holt and Company, 2017.

Slater, Michael D., and Donna Rouner. "Entertainment-Education and Elaboration Likelihood: Understanding the Processing of Narrative Persuasion." *Communication Theory* 12, no. 2 (2002): 173–91. doi:10.1111/j.1468-2885.2002.tb00265.x.

Smallwood, J. "Distinguishing How from Why the Mind Wanders: A process–Occurrence Framework for Self-Generated Mental Activity." *Psychological Bulletin* 139, no.3 (2013): 519–35. https://doi.org/10.1037/a0030010.

Smallwood, J., D. J. Fishman, and J. W. Schooler. "Counting the Cost of an Absent Mind: Mind Wandering as an Underrecognized Influence on Educational Performance." *Psychonomic Bulletin & Review* 14 (2007): 230–36. https://doi.org/10.3758/BF03194057.

Szpunar, Karl K., Samule T. Mounton, and Daniel L. Schacter. "Mind Wandering and Education: From the Classroom to Online Learning." Harvard Initiative for Teaching and Learning (2013).

Tversky, Amos, and Daniel Kahneman. "Judgment under Uncertainty: Heuristics and Biases."*Science*185,no.4157(1982):1124–131.doi:10.1017/cbo9780511809477.002.

Vezich, I. Stephanie, Perri L. Katzman, Daniel L. Ames, Emily B. Falk, and Matthew D. Lieberman. "Modulating the Neural Bases of Persuasion: Why/how, Gain/loss, and Users/non-users." *Social Cognitive and Affective Neuroscience* (2016). doi:10.1093/scan/nsw113.

Zak, Paul J. "The Neuroeconomics of Trust." *SSRN Electronic Journal*, 2005. doi:10.2139/ssrn.764944.

# Cafe Persuasion: The Micro-Pitch

Anderson, Janna, and Lee Rainie. "Millennials Will Benefit and Suffer Due to Their Hyperconnected Lives." Pew Research Center: Internet, Science & Tech, February 29, 2012. Accessed March 30, 2018. http://www.pewinternet.org/2012/02/29/millennials-will-benefit-and-suffer-due-to-their-hyperconnected-lives/.

Arnsten, A., and B. Li. "Neurobiology of Executive Functions: Catecholamine Influences on Prefrontal Cortical Functions." *Biological Psychiatry* (2004). doi:10.1016/j.bps.2004.08.019.

Arpan, Rhodes, and Roskos-Ewoldsen. "Chapter15: ATTITUDE ACCESSIBILITY: THEORY, METHODS AND FUTURE DIRECTIONS." In *Communication and Social Cognition: Theories and Methods*, edited by David R. Roskos-Ewoldsen and Jennifer L. Monahan. New York: Routledge, Taylor & Francis Group, 2013.

Blank, Steve. "How to Create an Elevator Pitch That Will Get You Funded." *Entrepreneur,* October 02, 2014. Accessed March 30, 2018. https://www.entrepreneur.com/article/237899.

Borzekowski, Dina L. G., and Thomas N. Robinson. "The 30-Second Effect." *Journal of the American Dietetic Association* 101, no. 1 (2001): 42–46. doi:10.1016/s0002-8223(01)00012-8.

Cialdini, Robert. *Pre-suasion: A Revolutionary Way to Influence and Persuade.* New York: Simon & Schuster, 2016.

Dieken, Connie. "Chapter 1: Why Connect? Attention Management." In *Talk Less, Say More 3 Habits to Influence Others and Make Things Happen*, 11–15. Hoboken: John Wiley & Sons, 2010.

Dillard, James Price, and Eugenia Peck. "Affect and Persuasion." *Communication Research* 27, no. 4 (2000): 461–95. doi:10.1177/009365000027004003.

Goss, Mimi. "Chapters 1 and 2." In *What Is Your One Sentence?: How to Be Heard in the Age of Short Attention Spans*, 9–24. New York: Prentice Hall Press, 2012.

Heath, Chip. "Chapters 1 and 2." In *Defining Moments*, 12–39. Bantam, 2017.

Hollerman, Jeffrey R., and Wolfram Schultz. "Dopamine Neurons Report an Error in the Temporal Prediction of Reward during Learning." *Nature Neuroscience* 1, no. 4 (1998): 304–09. doi:10.1038/1124.

Koordeman, Kuntsche, Doeschka J. Anschutz,van Baaren, and Rutger M. E. Engels. "Do We Act upon What We See? Direct Effects of Alcohol Cues in Movies on Young Adults' Alcohol Drinking." Alcohol and Alcoholism 46, no. 4 (2011): 393–98.

Lakoff, George, and Mark Johnson. *Metaphors We Live By.* Chicago: University of Chicago Press, 1980.

Lubars, David. 2017. https://www.ft.com/content/541f63d0-aa1a-11e7-93c5-648314d2c72c.

Mackey,John.https://archive.fortune.com/magazines/fortune/fortune_archive/2003/09/15/349175/index.htm.

McCormack, Joseph. *Brief: Make a Bigger Impact by Saying Less.* Hoboken, NJ: Wiley, 2014.

Miller, Fred E., and Charles Manion. *No Sweat! Elevator Speech: How to Craft Your Elevator Speech, Floor by Floor, with No Sweat!* St. Louis, MO: Fred, 2014

Nowak, Andrzej, and Robin R. Vallacher. "Dynamical Social Psychology: Finding Order in the Flow of Human Experience." In *Social Psychology: Handbook of Basic Principles*, edited by Arie W. Kruglanski and E. Tory Higgins, 30–32. New York: Guilford Press, 2007.

Pagliarini, Robert. "How to Write an Elevator Pitch." *Business Know-How,* November 10, 2017. Accessed March 25, 2018. https://www.businessknowhow.com/money/elevator.htm.

Postman, Neil. *Amusing Ourselves to Death: Public Discourse in the Age of Showbusiness.* London: Methuen, 2007.

Rideout, Vicky. "Measuring Time Spent with Media: The Common Sense Census of Media Use by US 8- to 18-year-olds." *Journal of Children and Media* 10, no. 1 (2016): 138–44. doi:10.1080/17482798.2016.1129808.

Schultz, Wolfram, Wiliam R. Stauffer, and Armin Lak. "The Phasic Dopamine Signal Maturing: From Reward via Behavioural Activation to Formal Economic Utility." *Current Opinion in Neurobiology* 43 (2017): 139–48. doi:10.1016/j.conb.2017.03.013.

Sillence, Elizabeth, Pam Briggs, Peter Richard Harris, and Lesley Fishwick. "How Do Patients Evaluate and Make Use of Online Health Information?" *Social Science & Medicine* 64, no. 9 (2007): 1853–862. doi:10.1016/j.socscimed.2007.01.012.

Sopory, Pradeep, and James Price Dillard. "The Persuasive Effects of Metaphor: A Meta-Analysis." *Human Communication Research* 28, no. 3 (2002): 382–419. doi:10.1111/j.1468-2958.2002.tb00813.x.

Ophir, E., C. Nass, and A. D. Wagner. "Cognitive Control in Media Multitaskers." *Proceedings of the National Academy of Sciences* 106, no. 37 (2009): 15583–5587. doi:10.1073/pnas.0903620106.

Van Patten, Jonathan. "Metaphors and Persuasion." *58 South Dakota Law Review* 295 (2013).

Weinreich, Harald, Hartmut Obendorf, Eelco Herder, and Matthias Mayer. "Not Quite the Average." *ACM Transactions on the Web* 2, no. 1 (2008): 1–31. doi:10.1145/1326561.1326566.

Whaley, Bryan B., and Austin S. Babrow. "Analogy in Persuasion: Translator's Dictionary or Art?" *Communication Studies* 44, nos. 3–4 (1993): 239–53. doi:10.1080/10510979309368398.

Yarrow, Kit. *Decoding the New Consumer Mind: How and Why We Shop and Buy.* Hoboken: Wiley, 2014.

## Your Face On the Street: Personal Branding

Gladwell, M. Blink: The Power of Thinking without Thinking. New York: Back Bay Books, 2019.

Neumeier, M. The Brand Gap. Berkeley, CA: New Riders, 2006.

Skagen, Peter. Your Public Speaking Superpower. Vancouver, BC: 2020.

## Kiosk: Sales Tools

Cialdini, Robert, Noah Goldstein, and Steve Martin. "Arizona Petrified Forest Study." *Yes: 50 Scientifically Proven Ways to Be Persuasive.* New York: Simon and Schuster, 2008.

Deci, Edward, and Richard Ryan. Handbook of Self-Determination Research, 2002. books.google.com. Self-Determination and Intrinsic Motivation in Human Behavior. 1985; 2001.

Freedman, J. L., and S. C. Fraser. "Compliance without Pressure: The Foot-in-the-Door Technique." *Journal of Personality and Social Psychology* 4, no. 2 (1966): 195–202. https://doi.org/10.1037/h0023552.

Lynn, Michael. "The Psychology of Unavailability: Explaining Scarcity and Cost Effects on Value." *Basic and Applied Social Psychology* 13, no. 1 (1992): 3–7. doi:10.1207/s15324834basp1301_2.

Mussweiler, T., and F. Strack. "Considering the Impossible: Explaining the Effects of Implausible Anchors." *Social Cognition* 19, no. 2 (2001): 145–60. doi:10.1521/soco.19.2.145.20705

Nielsen Survey. Social Proof. https://www.nielsen.com/ca/en/press-releases/2015/recommendations-from-friends-remain-most-credible-form-of-advertising/.

Strack, F., and T. Mussweiler. "Explaining the Enigmatic Anchoring Effect: Mechanisms of Selective Accessibility." Journal of Personality and Social Psychology 73, no. 3 (1997): 437–46. doi:10.1037/0022-3514.73.3.437.

Stanfield, Gayle M. "Incentives: The Effects on Reading Attitude and Reading Behaviors of Third-Grade Students," *The Corinthian* 9, no. 8 (2008). https://kb.gcsu.edu/thecorinthian/vol9/iss1/8.

Schwartz, E. *Breakthrough Advertising.* Westport, CT: Titans Marketing,

# Street Tools

Alvarez, Maria, "How Many Kinds of Reasons?" *Philosophical Explorations* 12, no. 2 (2009): 181–93, doi: 10.1080/13869790902838514.

Alvarez, Maria, "Reasons for Action: Justification, Motivation, Explanation." *The Stanford Encyclopedia of Philosophy* (Winter 2017 Edition), edited by Edward N. Zalta. https://plato.stanford.edu/archives/win2017/entries/reasons-just-vs-expl/.

Cialdini, R. B. *Pre-suasion: A Revolutionary Way to Influence and Persuade.* New York: Simon & Schuster Paperbacks, 2016.

Grenny, Joseph, Kerry Patterson, David Maxfield, Ron McMillan, and Al Switzler. *Influencer: The New Science of Leading Change.* North Ryde, NSW: McGraw-Hill, 2013.

Helliwell, John F., Lara B. Aknin, Hugh Shiplett, Haifang Huang, and Shun Wang. "Social Capital and Prosocial Behaviour as Sources of Well-Being." NBER Working Paper No. 23761. Issued in August 2017.

Hensrud, D. D. *Lose It. Mayo Clinic Diabetes Diet*, 2nd ed. (Revised and Updated). New York: RosettaBooks LLC, 2018.

Hughes, J. W., C. M. Goldstein, Carly Logan, Jessica L. Mulvany, Misty A. W. Hawkins, Amy F, Sato, amd John Gunstad. "Controlled Testing of Novel Portion Control Plate Produces Smaller Self-Selected Portion Sizes Compared To Regular Dinner Plate." *BMC Obesity* 4, no. 30 (2017). https://doi.org/10.1186/s40608-017-0167-z.

Kahneman, D., and I. Ritov. "Determinants of Stated Willingness to Pay for Public Goods: A Study in the Headline Method." *Journal of Risk and Uncertainty* 9 (1994): 5–37. https://doi.org/10.1007/BF01073401.

LU Xi, and Christopher K. Hsee. "Joint Evaluation versus Single Evaluation: A Field Full of Potentials." Acta Psychologica Sinica 50, no. 8 (2018): 827–39.

Mccroskey, James C., and Walter H. Combs. "The Effects of the Use of Analogy on Attitude Change and Source Credibility." *Journal of Communication* 19, no. 4 (1969): 333–39. doi:10.1111/j.1460-2466.1969.tb00856.x.

Redelmeier, D. A., and D. Kahneman. "Patients' Memories of Painful Medical Treatments: Real-Time And Retrospective Evaluations of Two Minimally Invasive Procedures." *Pain* 66, no. 1 (1996): 3–8. doi:10.1016/0304-3959(96)02994-6.

Sinek, S. *Start with Why: How Great Leaders Inspire Everyone to Take Action.* London: Portfolio Penguin, 2009. https://www.youtube.com/watch?v=HjriwYrGL28

Sopory, Pradeep, and James Price Dillard. "The Persuasive Effects of Metaphor: A Meta-Analysis." *Human Communication Research* 28, no. 3 (2002): 382–419. doi:10.1111/j.1468-2958.2002.tb00813.x.

Tversky, Amos, and Daniel Kahneman. "Judgment under Uncertainty: Heuristics and Biases."*Science*185,no.4157(1974):1124–131.doi:10.1017/cbo9780511809477.002.

Tversky, Amos, and Kahneman. "Judgment under Uncertainty: Heuristics and Biases." Science 185, no. 4157, (1999) 1124-131. doi:10.1017/cbo9780511809477.002.

Whaley, Bryan B., and Austin S. Babrow. "Analogy in Persuasion: Translator's Dictionary or Art?" *Communication Studies* 44, nos. 3–4 (1993): 239–53. doi:10.1080/10510979309368398.

# Street-Fight: Negotiate

https://www.masterclass.com/classes/chris-voss-teaches-the-art-of-negotiation/chapters/exercise-mirroring-and-labeling#

Kahneman, Daniel. Thinking, Fast and Slow. London: Allen Lane, 2011.

Voss, C. *Never Split the Difference*. London, UK: Cornerstone, 2017.

CPSIA information can be obtained
at www.ICGtesting.com
Printed in the USA
BVHW092002191222
654450BV00018B/157